# The Environmental Tradition

STUDIES IN THE ARCHITECTURE OF ENVIRONMENT

# Dean Hawkes

**E & FN SPON**
An Imprint of Chapman & Hall

London · Glasgow · Weinheim · New York · Tokyo
Melbourne · Madras

**Published by E & FN Spon,**
**an imprint of Chapman & Hall,**
**2–6 Boundary Row, London SE1 8HN, UK**

Chapman & Hall,
2–6 Boundary Row, London SE1 8HN, UK

Blackie Academic & Professional,
Wester Cleddens Road, Bishopbriggs,
Glasgow G64 2NZ, UK

Chapman & Hall GmbH,
Pappelallee 3, 69469 Weinheim, Germany

Chapman & Hall USA,
115 Fifth Avenue, New York, NY 10003, USA

Chapman & Hall Japan,
ITP-Japan, Kyowa Building, 3F, 2-2-1 Hirakawacho,
Chiyoda-ku, Tokyo 102, Japan

Chapman & Hall Australia,
102 Dodds Street, South Melbourne,
Victoria 3205, Australia

Chapman & Hall India,
R. Seshadri, 32 Second Main Road, CIT East,
Madras 600 035, India

First edition 1996

© 1996 Dean Hawkes

Typeset in 11/13 Garamond by Type Study, Scarborough
Printed in Great Britain by The Alden Press, Oxford

ISBN 0 419 19900 4

A catalogue record for this book is available from the British Library

# Contents

# Foreword

Leslie Martin and Lionel March, 'Fresnel' squares, comparison of courtyard and pavilion forms.

This book is about research in architecture, a subject that has recently come into prominence. Architecture departments are again required to show that they are actively pursuing research, as well as educating architects. I say 'again' because there is an aspect here of history repeating itself. After the Oxford Conference of 1958, sponsored by the Royal Institute of British Architects (RIBA) to examine the future of architectural education in the UK, *research* was the key concept by which leading practitioners thought that architectural education could free itself from the contingencies of professional life, and attempt to study recurring problems in buildings, in the environment and in the city. The RIBA had been brought to believe that architecture should be taught as a university subject. The university is about acquiring knowledge, not about exploiting professional know-how. If architecture is to be taught in the university, it must be thought of as a locus of research as well as the occasion of practice.

Among those leading practitioners two were important for architectural education: Richard Llewelyn Davies and Leslie Martin. Leslie Martin, who had come into prominence as the Architect to the London County Council, where he established new standards in public architecture, was appointed in 1956 to the first chair of architecture at Cambridge University, and transformed the Department of Architecture there. Llewelyn Davies was appointed to the Chair of Architecture at University College London in 1960, and his inaugural lecture *The Education of an Architect* established a new orientation towards research in architecture. Both men were reformers, and both became enormously influential in governmental and educational circles, but even more as mentors to younger architects impatient with the old establishment ways.

But there was a difference between them: Llewelyn Davies believed that research could only be scientific if carried out within the established categories of scientific research – that is, primarily looking for reasons in physical causality. 'Architecture' was a portmanteau word, not a category of thought, and architectural research was, effectively, a part of Building Science. Martin, on the other hand, believed that 'architecture' had a separate existence, at least as an established tradition, and that research could be carried out into specifically architectural fields, and by architects.

Both men set up research frameworks at their respective architecture schools and attracted research contracts. The difference between them became in itself a useful point in considering what research could be undertaken. It could be read as a choice between architects becoming scientists, and scientists becoming architects.

Both directions were valid. But there was, among many architects, a special sense of jubilation when Leslie Martin formalized research at Cambridge under the title 'Land Use and Built Form Studies'. This declared, at the outset, that key aspects of architecture could only be researched by identifying their architectural potential. And as buildings occupy land, there exists a basic geometry which relates built form to land use. Research in this zone is both mathematical and, in the mathematical sense, factual. But it is also architectural.

In an important address to architects at the RIBA in 1987, Martin brought to their notice the research he had already carried out on the relationship between density and building form. He focussed on the famous case of the Fresnel square, where a thin annulus at the outer edge has the same area as a stout square at the centre; by the same geometry a peripheral ring of two-storey houses could have the same density as a single tower block, for the same site area. By studying answers, new insights could be gained into problems. This was prescient, for computer analysis deals as effectively with answers as with problems. Essentially, Martin was anticipating the scientist Herbert Simon, who in 1969 proposed to put alongside the natural sciences 'the sciences of the artificial', in order to study the intricate forms produced by man, whether as language or as forms of thought.

When put together with his love of rational geometries, whether in urban grids or in enclosed courtyards, and his distaste for tower blocks, this approach condensed as a love of architecture. Martin gathered around him people of talent, both architects and scientists. Theorists like Rowe, Eisenman and Echenique, architects like March, Hodgkinson and his successor to the Chair of Architecture, Colin St John Wilson. He set up no artificial opposition between the invention of architectural form and the rational analysis of what had been invented: in his view practical reason led on into speculative reason, without a break. Through a numerous progeny that have taken his assumptions as their starting point, Martin has had an enormous influence on architecture, as well as on architectural education, practice and research.

The Centre for Land Use and Built Form Studies soon became the Martin Centre. Today it no longer concentrates only on the geometry of land use, but promotes a wide range of research activities that takes in functional planning, environmental design, energy studies, acoustics, transportation, earthquake resistance, intermediate technology and computer studies, along with a spin-off of useful consultancies. In a sense, Llewelyn Davies' wider throw has been vindicated. However, in the extended history of the Martin Centre, what has been vindicated there, beyond doubt, is the humanist approach which Leslie Martin originally introduced, where dogma is to be avoided and reason quietly applied to answers as well as to problems.

For this wide range of research activities is incapable in itself of providing a balanced overview of architectural practice, still less a theory of architecture. In the 1960s, we did not fully appreciate the intricacy of human thought, the difficulty of reducing it to linear analysis. Today, we need more than ever to combine, as Leslie Martin advocated, practical reason with speculative reason.

Dean Hawkes was associated with scientific research at Cambridge from 1965, and was one of the co-founders of the Centre for Land Use and Built Form Studies. He was Director of the Martin Centre from 1979 to 1987, and Joint Director from 1987 to 1993. But he has also been a fully participating member of the School of Architecture, as a University Lecturer in Architecture, and of the University, as a Fellow of Darwin College. He is also a practising architect. From this balanced experience he has developed a view of how science and architectural design can work together for their mutual benefit. He clearly understands the relationship Martin propounded between practical reason and speculative reason.

The present book is squarely based on this understanding. In these essays, Dean Hawkes follows closely wherever scientific analysis can have a direct effect on building form, sometimes at a fundamental level, sometimes incidental. But he never oversimplifies in the attempt to assert a general theory of scientific design. He is thoroughly conscious of the loose fit, that architects know only too well, between form and performance: a space in which cultural pressures can produce strange distortions. He thus balances in his own thinking the insights of a scientist and the propensities of an architect, and we benefit from this understanding.

He also evinces a respect for architecture as a discipline that seems to me to correspond closely with the love of architecture that we sense in Leslie Martin.

Robert Maxwell
London
August
1995

# Acknowledgements

These essays were originally written in the small gaps which, from time to time, have almost miraculously appeared in the midst of a life preoccupied with the demands of full-time teaching, the conduct of funded research projects and active participation in the work of a small, but busy architectural practice.

Upon reflection these small gaps have almost always been fashioned by others, through their invitations to contribute to conferences or write essays for journals. I am, therefore, indebted to all of those who, in this way, have given me these opportunities to step outside my other obligations and, thus, to maintain an engagement with broader themes. I should like to thank the sequence of editors and others at the *Architects' Journal* in London who, for over 20 years, have asked me to look at and write about buildings of immense diversity of type, scale and situation. I owe a great debt of gratitude for this to four editors, Leslie Fairweather, Peter Carolin, Colin Davies and Stephen Greenberg, and, for a long period as buildings editor, Patrick Hannay. I must add further thanks to Peter Carolin for his continued support for my activities since he left the *AJ* and became head of the Department of Architecture at Cambridge and to Stephen Greenberg who, before he became the editor of the *AJ* in 1991, was my partner in the practice of Greenberg and Hawkes.

Many of the thoughts presented in this book were first tested upon students and colleagues in Cambridge and I have learned much from their critical responses. I have also benefited beyond measure from the wider conversation which takes place, both publicly and privately in the department and which has constantly helped to shape my thinking. Over the years I have particularly welcomed the influence of Lionel March, Bill Howell, Nick Bullock, Hayden Willey, Diane Haigh, Nick Baker and Koen Steemers and, as a constant presence, Leslie Martin.

The production of the book has been helped by the efforts of Andrew Mead in picture research and Claude Demers and Andre Potvin who have redrawn many of the original figures to ensure some graphical consistency. Finally, I should like to record my gratitude to my editor, Caroline Mallinder, without whose ability to conjure up and keep me to deadlines the whole enterprise would have foundered.

Dean Hawkes
Cambridge
1995

# Introduction

1
The 'Strip' at Las Vegas, USA.

With the publication, in 1969, of *The Architecture of the Well-tempered Environment*,[1] Reyner Banham restored the environmental function of buildings to its rightful position as a fundamental concern of architectural theory and practice. It is curious that, as the technologies of environmental control evolved through the nineteenth and twentieth centuries, this historic function of all buildings was progressively relegated to a secondary place in the discourse. In the schools of architecture it was found as a branch of building science, relying for its substance upon the achievements of the building scientists in quantifying the environmental problem – be it of heat, light or sound – and in practice it had effectively been handed over to the emerging profession of mechanical and electrical consultants.

In his account, Banham explained the role played by environmental technologies and visions in defining the nature of the modern movement. But this was given little or no recognition in the earlier standard histories such as those by Nikolaus Pevsner or J.M. Richards.[2] Writing in the late 1960s Banham could not anticipate the impact of the so-called energy crisis that was to follow in the early 1970s. The environmental history he developed was, in many respects, a record of the progressive increase in the energy consumption of buildings. At the close of the book he drew out, with great foresight, alternative futures through either the 'power-operated' or the 'conservative' mode of environmental control, but he offered no clear judgement about the virtues or vices of either. The attractions of a totally power-operated environment, such as the Las Vegas Strip (Figure 1), were as potent for him as the sober virtues of St George's School at Wallasey (Figure 2). The energy crisis, whether it was perceived as a matter of physical global survival or as purely a matter of geopolitics, helped to change all our attitudes to building environment, not, perhaps, in the broad cultural sense in which Banham approached it, but by beginning to redress the balance of the relative roles played by the fabric and mechanical systems of buildings. From this came new insights and solutions which contributed much to the development of theory and practice from the mid-1970s to mid-1990s.

The essays collected together in this book were written in just these decades and, while they were produced for many reasons, may together constitute a commentary on the significance of the environmental dimension of architecture during this period. To set them in context it is necessary to step back a little and try to establish some wider themes than any of them individually can be expected to present.

**The Vitruvian model**

The earliest extensive account of environmental design in architecture is to be found in Vitruvius' *Ten Books on Architecture*.[3] In

Book I, Chapter IV, on 'The site of a city', and Chapter VI, on 'The directions of the streets', both emphasize the importance of environmental factors. In Book VI, we find what remains one of the most eloquent statements on the subject when, in describing houses for different regions, Vitruvius wrote,

In the north, houses should be entirely roofed over and sheltered as much as possible, not in the open, though having a warm exposure. But, on the other hand, where the force of the sun is great in the southern countries that suffer from heat, houses must be built more in the open and with a northern or north-eastern exposure. Thus we may amend by art what nature, if left to herself, would mar.

Later in Book VI, Vitruvius discusses 'The proper exposures of the different rooms' and, by implication, defines expectations of comfort when he speaks of the purposes of bedrooms and libraries requiring the morning light and, hence, an eastern exposure. These fundamental relationships between climate, comfort and the role of architecture may be described by the 'Vitruvian tri-partite model of environment' (Figure 3).

This model, in its great simplicity, is sufficient to describe the nature of environmental control as exercised by buildings for many centuries, in which the building's fabric, its architecture, was the primary agent of mediation between the external and internal environments. With the industrial revolution, however, the emergence of new sources of power, and of the means to harness and deliver them, began the process of transformation which Banham was one of the first to record.

In analytical terms this was recognized by another significant author of the 1960s, Victor Olgyay, in his book *Design with Climate*.[4] In this he proposed a model of the environmental process which, allowing for its 1960s' terminology, is simply a development of the Vitruvian model, extended to include the function of 'technology', of plant and systems, in the environmental scheme of modern buildings (Figure 4).

In Olgyay, however, we find an anticipation of what became known as 'bioclimatic architecture' in the clear commitment, made explicit in the very title of the book, to environmental control achieved through working with, rather than against, climate. His diagram, which shows the distinct steps in proceeding from the varying climate to the stable condition of comfort, is a lucid model of the environmental design process (Figure 5). Olgyay's work is a rare instance of an effective synthesis of building science with architecture. In his invention of the 'schematic bioclimatic index' he provided an analytical system by which the relationship of climate to comfort may be clearly established for any given conditions (Figure 6). Then, through his simple taxonomy of building types related to climate (Figure 7), it is possible to initiate the development of an appropriate design. The use of the idea of 'type' in the development of designs has been a significant aspect of the theoretical debate in architecture, and has particular value in the field of environmental design. This subject is addressed in a number of the essays that follow.

## Towards a theory of environmental control

The essays are arranged into two groups. The first is concerned with theoretical aspects of environmental design and the second is a series of critical reviews of buildings. A quarter of a century ago there was little which could be said to be a theory of environmental design. Building science operated on a platform, primarily derived from physics, to provide a means for the calculation of quantities of heat, light and sound in buildings, but there was no comprehensive theory of the environmental processes that are at work in buildings. In the early 1970s the architecture department in Cambridge set out to develop a model of the 'environmental system' of buildings.[5] Conceived very much in the spirit of the time, when many

2
Emslie A. Morgan, St George's School, Wallesey, 1961.

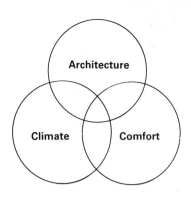

**3**
Vitruvian tri-partite model of
environment.

**4**
Interlocking fields of climate balance.

**5**
Flattening the temperature curve from
environmental conditions (1) by
microclimatology (2) and climate balance
of the structure (3) to mechanical heating
or cooling (4).

disciplines in the humanities were exploring the potential of descriptive models, this used ideas from dynamic systems theory and, in particular, the work of J.W. Forrester[6] to construct a representation of the sources, flows and destinations of the energy used in buildings. It also, and of crucial importance, represented the means by which these were monitored and controlled.

The first essay in this book, 'The theoretical basis of comfort in "selective" environments', includes a summary of the structure of this model and also makes a fundamental distinction between approaches to environmental control in contemporary practice. In *The Architecture of the Well-tempered Environment*, Banham suggested that historic buildings fall into three distinct 'modes' of environmental control: the 'conservative', the 'selective' and the 'regenerative'. In this essay the 'selective' and 'exclusive' modes

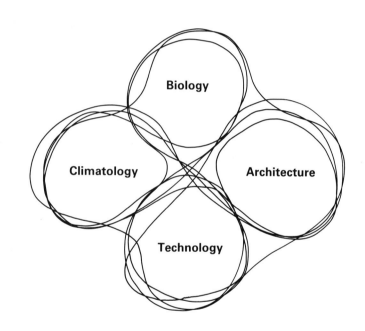

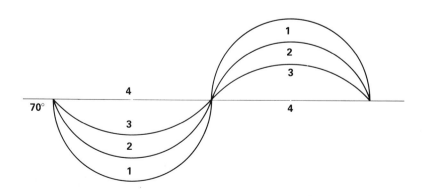

rework Banham's terms to make clear the difference between buildings that use ambient energy sources in creating natural environments and those that rely predominantly upon mechanical plant to create controlled, artificial environments. The central argument is that the users of buildings are capable of exercising sophisticated and effective control over their environments if they are given the opportunity. In developing this argument the essay contradicted much of the conventional wisdom of design practice which was, at the time, dominated by the belief that the 'interference' of the users compromised the quality of the internal environment and led to increased energy use.

The essay placed second here, 'Building shape and energy use', continues the discussion of 'selective' and 'exclusive' design, and gives particular emphasis to the connection between environmental design and architectural form. This shows that the logical consequence of the 'exclusive' mode, with its overriding concern to isolate the internal environment from the exterior, is to restrict the form and nature of the building envelope. The ultimate 'exclusive' building is a squat, deep-plan form with a highly insulated exterior with minimal openings. A 'selective' design, on the other hand, has a more complex form and its envelope has greater transparency and complexity because it admits and controls ambient energy sources. During the twentieth century, mechanical and electrical service systems reached a state of development at which they could replace all of the elements of the natural environment in buildings. At this moment the essential nature of architecture was fundamentally challenged. The historical struggle of all buildings to connect inside to outside could be replaced by the flick of a switch. The distinction of 'selective' and 'exclusive' lays bare the issue.

A wider background to this argument is set out in 'Types, norms and habit in environmental design'. Here, the importance of the idea of 'type' in the initiation of the process of design is demonstrated through a review of the evolution of the British office building. This shows that there is a tendency for environmental design practice to be dominated by the influence of the prevailing 'stereotype', which fundamentally preconditions the outcome of the design process. The essay argues that it is more productive if reference is made, not to a single type, but to the accumulated store of solutions. This opens up the prospect of making a connection between the problems of environmental design, with their conventional reliance upon technical concepts, and architectural history – an idea pursued in more depth in the following essay, 'Precedent and theory in the design of auditoria'.

Since its foundations in the work of W.C. Sabine at the turn of the century,[7] modern architectural acoustics has become one of the most successful branches of building science. The branch that attracts most notice and comment is concerned with the design of

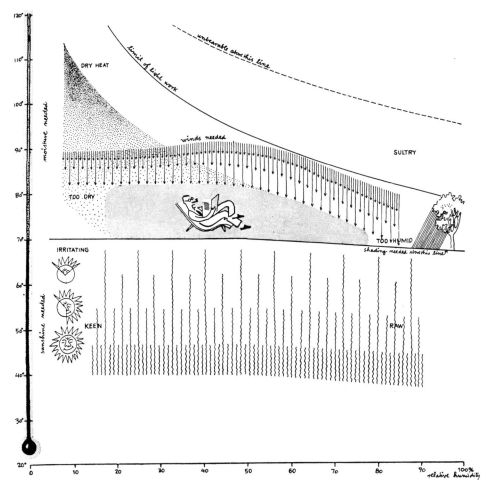

auditoria, of concert halls and opera houses. The aim of this essay is to examine, through the specific case of auditorium design, the question of the potential of the mathematical abstractions of building science directly to influence the production of architectural form. The evidence shows that, after almost a century of scientific development, the substantive basis for effective auditorium design remains historical precedent.

'Objective knowledge and the art and science of architecture' rounds off this discussion of environmental design, type and design method by reviewing arguments that have played a part in the thought of the Cambridge School, which Leslie Martin established in the 1950s. This proposes a connection between the work of the architectural theoretician, W.R. Lethaby, and the evolutionary standpoint of Karl Popper's 'objective knowledge', as a means of furthering the relationship between the worlds of history, design theory and practice in architecture.

The distinction between the 'selective' and 'exclusive' modes is

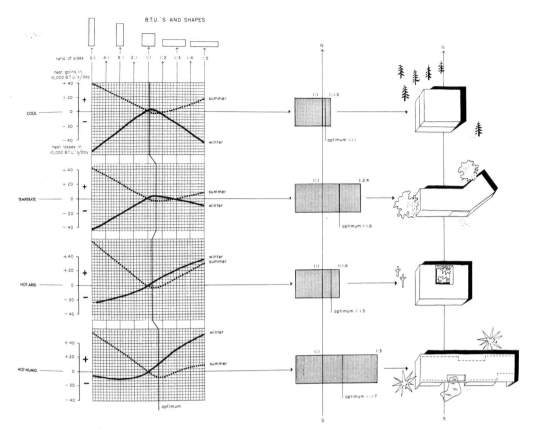

principally concerned with the nature of the relationship between the internal and external environments. There is, however, as Banham revealed, a second significant strand to the environmental transformation of architecture in the twentieth century. This is the question of the growth of reliance upon mechanical service systems, part of the move to the 'exclusive', and the corresponding need to find a place for them. 'Space for services: the architectural dimension' presents an alternative view to Banham's in which it is argued that the expansion of service systems does not necessarily demand elaborate and explicit architectural display. The proposition is based upon consideration of the extent of services in many nineteenth-, and even eighteenth-, century buildings in which the stylistic preoccupations of the time continued without compromise or contradiction while bulky services were threaded through their fabric. This leads to the discussion of the relationship between environmental technology and language in architecture in the essay, 'The language barrier'. This resists claims for a technological determinism, whether they originate in the celebration of the machinery of environmental control, or in the apparently benign

17 | Introduction

calls for a 'new architecture', which come from some quarters of the environmental lobby.

'Environment at the threshold' takes a broad look at the theoretical arguments developed in the preceding essays and moves on to propose a programme for research and practice in environmental design. The essence of this revolves around the transition that occurred from the technologically dominated attitudes of the 1960s and 1970s – as represented in built form by the deep-plan, air-conditioned office building stereotype, and in theoretical terms by the 'exclusive' mode – to the humanistic, environmentally responsible approaches of the bioclimatic, 'selective' mode. Central to this is the idea of environmental diversity, realized and experienced spatially and temporally. This envisages spaces in which environmental uniformity, in all its dimensions of heat, light and sound, is replaced by variations, within limits, which maintain, in the occupant, a sense of the dynamics of the natural climate, of the proper condition of humankind.

The first part of the book concludes with an examination of 'The Cambridge School and the environmental tradition'. Beginning with the work of the school's founder, Edward Prior, this essay shows how environmental concerns have consistently played a role in the buildings of architects associated with the Cambridge School of Architecture. The essay offers a further development of the 'selective'/'exclusive' theme, in which a diagram of the 'three magnets of environment' – with apologies to Ebenezer Howard – proposes a third category, the 'pragmatic'. It also discusses the construction of a 'taxonomy of selective design', which makes an explicit connection between selective concepts and the use of type in the production of building designs. The essay concludes by building upon the classical urban theory of Johann Heinrich von Thünen, in his model of the 'isolated state', to look forward towards the prospect of a city whose buildings move from consumption to the production of energy.

### Theory into practice

One of the defining characteristics of architecture as a discipline is the complex interrelation between theory and practice. In many ways the situation is analogous to that in music as described by Igor Stravinsky. In the collection of *Conversations with Igor Stravinsky* his reply to the question, 'what is theory in musical composition?' was characteristically succinct:

Hindsight. It doesn't exist. There are compositions from which it is deduced. Or, if this isn't true, it has a by-product existence that is powerless to create or even to justify. Nevertheless, composition involves a deep intuition of theory.[8]

In architecture, as in music, there are circumstances in which practice may be informed by theory, but, equally, there are others in which significant developments in the theoretical foundation of the discipline follow from the work of practitioners.

In *The Architecture of the Well-tempered Environment*, Banham's contribution to theory rests upon the commentary he develops on the work of architects and, in some cases, of engineers. Since the 1970s I have been privileged to write a series of critical essays on current building practice for the *Architects' Journal*. Many of these are studies of buildings in which questions of environmental control are of fundamental significance in their conception. Those reprinted here have been chosen to illustrate both the importance these questions assumed in the practice of this period and something of the nature of the relationship between theory and practice.

St George's School at Wallasey was, for Banham, writing in 1969, a significant signpost to the future. In juxtaposing it with the 'power-operated' extreme of Las Vegas, 'an environment defined in light without visible structure of any consequence', he drew attention to its significance for the future of environmental design. Writing in 1987, I had the benefit of access to the meticulous research into the performance of the school undertaken by Dr Davies of the University of Liverpool.[9] This shows just how the balance between the energy supplied by the solar wall and that from the occupants and the electric lights work together to maintain thermal comfort throughout the year in the temperate, but not obviously sunny, climate of northwest England. This evidence confirms the accuracy of Banham's description of the building and its operation. He was, however, totally incorrect in his assertion that the original auxiliary heating system had been removed when it became apparent that it was superfluous. As Davies' reports show, it remains in place and, on rare occasions, has been used.

It is poetic justice that this building, which was disregarded, and in some instances vilified, by the education establishment, has now acquired iconic status, fully justifying the commitment and vision of its architect Emslie Morgan. An inheritor of its lessons is Netley Abbey Infants' School, built in 1984 by the Architect's Department of Hampshire County Council, under the direction of Colin Stansfield Smith. In this case the designers turned to research to help them develop an approach to low-energy school design, working with the group at Cambridge of which I was a member. Here was a case in which theory and practice were explicitly brought into collaboration, with successful results, as confirmed by the performance of the building. With its combination of passive solar techniques and user controls over the plant and environmental control elements of the building envelope, this building was the first built embodiment of the principles of 'selective design'.

Throughout recent history the office building has been at the centre of developments in environmental design. In its transformation from the counting house to the modern business centre it has consistently exploited the latest technologies of mechanical servicing to sustain the goal of efficiency. In one sense it may be argued that the air-conditioned glass skyscraper is the most successful production of the construction industry in the twentieth century. Following the inspiration and ideology of Mies van der Rohe's projects for glass skyscrapers in Berlin of 1919 (Figure 8) and 1922, its very presence in every city of the developed world, regardless of the climate, symbolizes the ability of technology to overcome nature. Within the overall economy of the multinational corporations, which are the most frequent occupants of skyscrapers, the extravagant use of energy which these structures inevitably require is rarely important. In spite of this, some of the most interesting contributions to the development of an alternative vision of environmental design have been made through office design.

In the 1970s the Electricity Council in Britain promoted an approach to environmental design that it labelled 'Integrated Environmental Design' (IED). In its most literal manifestations this was the ultimate instance of the 'exclusive' mode. Squat, deep-plan buildings had highly insulated, minimally glazed exterior walls and the mechanical plant recovered heat from the permanently used artificial lighting to eliminate the need for a heating system. The buildings did, however, have cooling plant to deal with overheating on all but the coldest days. IED was marketed as a means of obtaining all the 'benefits' of full air conditioning at lower capital cost than a conventional building with heating and cooling plant, and with some savings in running costs. Behind the wide-eyed claims of environmental virtue lay a hidden agenda in which the aim was to obtain a larger share of the office environment market and, perhaps more important, to help spread the demand for electricity more evenly over the year. This would then allow the power-generation industry to achieve greater efficiency in the operation of its plant than was possible with a high seasonal fluctuation of demand with its peak occurring in the winter months.

Against this background Arup Associates' design for the regional headquarters building for the Central Electricity Generating Board at Bedminster Down near Bristol, completed in 1979, was remarkable in many respects. The clients began the conversation with their architects with the requirement that the building should be a further demonstration of IED principles. But Arup achieved a transformation of the arid stereotype. The practice accepted the general idea that the building should be a complete system in which building envelope and mechanical systems work in harmonious relationship. But Arup redefined and refined the nature and function of the envelope so that natural light was restored and it

8
Mies van der Rohe, glass skyscraper project, Berlin, 1919.

became possible to use natural ventilation by opening windows. These moves led to the production of a seminal design, which was to have wide influence at the time.

In a later building, Gateway Two at Basingstoke of 1983, Arup Associates made another important contribution to the evolution of the office building. In a short article published in 1978, Richard MacCormac and I reported on simple research investigations in which we had examined the environmental potential of buildings organized around glazed courtyards.[10] These studies, which had their origins in the work on the land use potential of pavilion and courtyard forms undertaken at Cambridge in the 1960s by Leslie Martin and Lionel March,[11] showed that these structures could provide year-round comfort in office buildings in the British climate with great economy of energy use. Arup's building, with its elegant central atrium – a feature that became one of the dominant themes, if not to say clichés, of office building design throughout the world in the 1980s – was a total realization of the theoretical arguments. Unlike so many other atrium office buildings it has no air conditioning, except in a small area of computer room, and achieves natural ventilation for the entire building by exploiting the natural buoyancy of warm air rising up the atrium. The building has been a great influence on the low-energy architecture movement, inspiring not only practice but academic research.

In 1863 Florence Nightingale published her *Notes on Hospitals* and, thereby, established the idea that the physical environment found in hospital buildings should be regarded positively as an essential element of the healing process. In the modern hospital this principle continues to be upheld and, in its realization, these buildings have become extremely complex. In *The Architecture of the Well-tempered Environment* Banham wrote at great length about Henman and Cooper's design for the Royal Victoria Hospital in Belfast, completed in 1903 (Figure 9). This employed a system of mechanical ventilation which allowed it to adopt a compact plan form. The wards were lit through continuous rooflights, a development which was prophetic of the progressive mechanization of the hospital environment which has occurred in the twentieth century.

By the 1970s the energy costs of this mechanization were becoming a significant burden upon the National Health Service in Britain. Following a series of research studies into the energy demands and processes of the modern hospital, the design for St Mary's Hospital on the Isle of Wight, by Ahrends, Burton & Koralek, addressed the question of how to create a high standard of environment economically. In doing this the building, completed in 1982, was one of the first, and certainly one of the most complex, demonstrations of the application of low-energy design principles to be realized in Britain.

The Italian architect and academic Sergio Los has, throughout his

9
Henman and Cooper, Royal Victoria Hospital, Belfast, 1903.

10
Sergio Los, Kindergarten at Crossara,
1972.

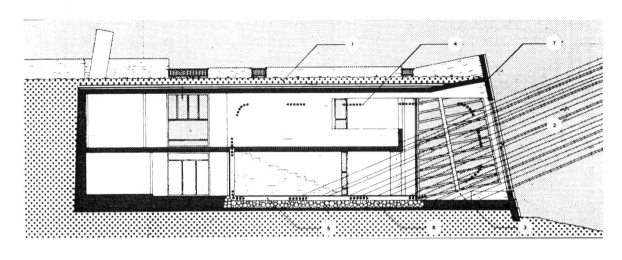

11
Andrea Palladio, Villa Rotonda,
Vicenza, c. 1550.

12
Colen Campbell, Mereworth Castle,
1725.

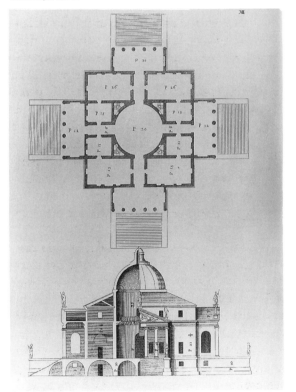

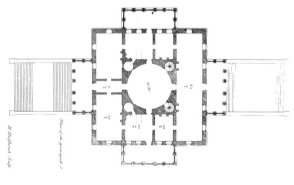

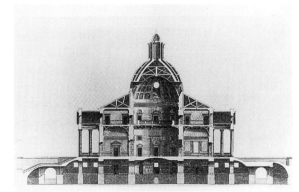

career, combined research and writing on themes of environmental design, 'bioclimatic design' as he prefers to call it, with practice. His buildings consistently address the difficult question of the synthesis of his environmental interests with the broader themes of contemporary architectural theory. The building for Cassa Rurale e Artigianale at Brendola in northern Italy was completed in 1990 and is the most elaborate and explicit demonstration of his investigations. In earlier buildings, such as the Kindergarten at Crossara of 1972 (Figure 10), the language is modernist with the large conservatory, which is the principal element of the building's energy strategy, clearly differentiated, in form and material, from the body of the building. In this it is comparable with the Wallasey School, where the logic of Morgan's analytical approach to the collection of solar energy is the source of the building's characteristic wedge-shaped section, high to the south and low to the north. At Brendola, however, the objectives are more ambitious. Here the juxtapositions are more complex, with urban context, functional organization, environmental design, the ordering of structure, enclosure and services systems, and historical reference all playing a part in the development of the design.

This concern to discover a richer and, perhaps, more elaborate order as the basis for the production of architecture has been one of the central themes of the theoretical debate during the years since Banham wrote *The Architecture of the Well-tempered Environment*. A building which exemplifies this, and which is also most profoundly concerned with environmental design, is the Crystallographic Data Centre at Cambridge by the Danish architect Erik Sørensen, completed in 1992. The difference between the climate of the Veneto and that of southern England was clearly expressed in the nature of the transformations which Andrea Palladio's great models underwent in the hands of the English neo-Palladians. A comparison between the Villa Rotonda and Colen Campbell's Mereworth (Figures 11 and 12) shows how the dominant preoccupation with summer heat in Italy is replaced by the northern European concern for warmth in winter. This is most clearly revealed by the greater subdivision of Campbell's interior and the provision of no fewer than 24 fireplaces, all located in the masonry core of the rotunda.

In strictly environmental terms the most striking contrast between Los' and Sørensen's buildings is found in the design of their rooflights, in which this historic distinction continues to be manifest. At Brendola, in response to Italian light and heat, these are relatively small and have permanent, external shading devices. They serve primarily to light the central circulation and meeting spaces. In temperate Cambridge an enormous, south-facing scoop rises above the flat roof to bring daylight down into the heart of the building. Beneath this Sørensen creates a sophisticated, but naturally lit and ventilated, contemporary working environment for computer-based research. He also constructs a metaphorical nature, in the form of an internal garden and a crystal-forming pool set into the first floor. Close to this an inglenook with an open fire is an alternative environment for the researchers and a memory of the primal sheltering function of architecture.

The design of the modern art museum is dominated by concerns for the conservation of works of art. This has become a highly specialized and technical environmental challenge in which temperature, humidity and light levels must be strictly controlled to protect the displayed and stored artefacts. The two concluding essays, Robert Venturi and Denise Scott Brown's Sainsbury Wing extension to the National Gallery in London of 1991, and the American gallery designs by Louis Kahn, reflect something of the shifting priorities in the architectural debate during the last quarter of a century. They also, more specifically, cast a particular light on the question of environmental technology and architectural language.

In his buildings at Yale University in 1953, Fort Worth in 1972 and back again at Yale in 1974, Kahn produced three entirely different solutions. Working with the specific circumstances of each project, of programme, site and climate, he created a sequence of designs that serve as potent models. The Yale Art Gallery, New Haven, is, perhaps, most significant for the development of the tetrahedral structure of the slabs, through which the services were threaded. At the Kimbell Art Museum, Fort Worth, the alternation of major and minor, served and servant, bays is another solution to the problem of the location of services, which keeps the vaults of the major bays free to become the light source. At the Mellon Center at Yale University, New Haven, the adoption of V-section structural beams allows the structural and service zones to be centred on the square grid. A rooflight system of the utmost simplicity provides controlled and beautiful light. In each building the technical solution is clearly visible and becomes, thereby, a vital element of the language. All three buildings are both functional and symbolic.

This relationship of function and symbol has long been a central theme in Robert Venturi's theoretical and critical writings. In his and Denise Scott Brown's design for the Sainsbury Wing they set out to avoid the contradiction of creating what they had, in *Learning from Las Vegas* defined as 'non-functioning functional elements' by making direct reference to historical precedent.[12] The changed requirements of environmental control make it necessary, however, to encase this adaptation of the cross-section of Sir John Soane's Dulwich Picture Gallery in London, 1814, in a cocoon of rooftop structures and mechanical plant.

This comparison suggests a further development of the distinc-

**Notes and references**

1
Banham, R., *The Architecture of the Well-tempered Environment*, Architectural Press, London, 1969.

2
Pevsner, N., *Pioneers of Modern Design*, Pelican Books, Harmondsworth, 1960; Richards, J.M., *An Introduction to Modern Architecture*, Penguin Books, Harmondsworth, 1940.

3
Vitruvius, *Ten Books on Architecture*, Morgan, M.H. (trans.), Dover, New York, 1960.

4
Olgyay, V., *Design with Climate*, Princeton University Press, Princeton, 1963.

5
Hawkes, D. and Willey, H., 'User response in the environmental control system', *Transactions of the Martin Centre for Architectural and Urban Studies*, vol. 2, Woodhead-Faulkner, Cambridge, 1977.

6
Forrester, J.W., *Principles of Systems*, Wright-Allen Press, Cambridge, Mass., 1968.

7
Sabine, W.C., *Collected Papers on Acoustics*, Hunt, F. (ed.), Dover, New York, 1964.

8
Stravinsky, I. and Craft, R., *Conversations with Igor Stravinsky*, Faber Music, London, 1959.

9
Dr M. Davies of the University of Liverpool published a group of papers describing the performance of the Wallasey School in considerable detail in the journal *Energy Research* in 1987.

10
Hawkes, D. and MacCormac, R., 'Office form and energy use', *RIBA Journal*, June 1978.

11
Martin, L. and March, L., 'Built form and land use', *Cambridge Research*, April 1966.

12
Venturi, R., Scott Brown, D. and Izenour, S., *Learning from Las Vegas*, MIT Press, Cambridge, Mass., 1972.

tion between the 'selective' and 'exclusive' modes. Kahn's buildings, even though they, of necessity, incorporate sophisticated mechanical systems, retain a fundamental connection between the internal and external environments. It was Kahn, after all, who wrote that 'a room is not a room without natural light'. In this respect they are 'selective' designs. Venturi's building achieves an almost complete isolation of the two environments and is, thus, 'exclusive'.

# Part One

# Theory

# 1 The theoretical basis of comfort in 'selective' environments

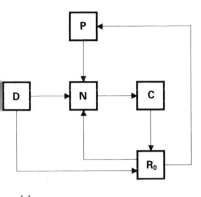

1.1
Environmental control, minimal system.

1.2
The primitive hut, after Laugier.

Until quite recently the theory and practice of environmental control in buildings did not take into account the nature of the voluntary responses of building occupants to the environmental conditions they experience. To some degree this neglect was a reflection of the complexity of the subject, but was also a consequence of the predominant view of the aims and methods of environmental control. In this, the desired environment is specified as a series of precise statements about temperature, ventilation rate, illumination levels and so forth. These are maintained within quite narrow limits and this usually means, in practice, that reliance is placed upon mechanical systems which are, in turn, subjected to automatic control.

The historical influences upon the theory and practice of environmental control have been set out at some length.[1] These can be seen to have followed a series of logical steps along a line of development established by the paradigms of building science and of the modern movement in architecture, with their respective concerns with scientific precision and of a definite, if not definitive, relationship between form and function.

The validity of these assumptions has been questioned in recent years, a notable 'early warning' being that issued by Musgrove in 1966.[2] As part of this critique, a conceptual model of the environmental system in architecture was developed.[3] This led directly to an investigation of the response of the occupants of five primary school buildings to the different, and differing, environments they experienced. Analysis of the results of this work led to the definition of a distinction between the exclusive and selective modes of environment.

Further work set out a series of rudimentary propositions about the nature of a selective building and the kind of environment it might offer.[4] These were subsequently developed and found concrete expression in a design for a primary school to be constructed at Locksheath in Hampshire.[5]

**The environmental system**

If we take an evolutionary view of humanity's attempts to control the environment we can begin by describing the situation of humans in nature (Figure 1.1). Using terminology from the theory of cybernetics, in this Figure, D is a set of environmental disturbances which impinge upon a person, C is the set of physiological variables which determine the person's state of comfort, N is the channel through which D is transmitted to C and is, in effect, a combination of the physical environment and the individual's physiology. The precise state of N will depend upon certain parameters such as geographical location and body posture and these are represented by P. Even in this minimal system there are some opportunities for control and this is indicated by the regulating term RO.

Primitive humanity's adoption of clothing and shelter, the primitive hut beloved of architectural theoreticians (Figure 1.2), may be represented by the next development of the diagram (Figure 1.3). The new terms are F, which in cybernetics terminology is a filter and, in this particular case, can be taken to be the fabric of the building; I is a description of the internal environment; N becomes N' to represent the effects of clothing and P' allows for the wider range of parameters now available as a result of the variability of both clothing and the building fabric.

In our evolutionary account the benefits of shelter are soon augmented by the introduction of 'plant', M (Figure 1.4). This adds further parameters to the system, P'', and is subjected to regulation by the occupant, even if, in the primitive case, this would amount to no more than adding wood to the fire! A complete picture of the system that is possible in a modern building is achieved by adding automatic controls on plant and fabric (Figure 1.5).

In diagrammatic form we now have a broad representation of the full range of possibilities of environmental control in buildings. Clearly, the reality in any practical building is much more complex. The possible combinations of form, construction and plant are numerous and the environment itself has many dimensions of heat, light and sound. The value of the model is that it provides us with a framework within which we may describe and classify approaches to control. If we translate the abstract terminology of this model into the language of building we can illustrate the essential difference between the exclusive and selective modes of control.

In seeking to gain a deeper understanding of the subject four questions were posed:

1.3
Environmental control augmented by clothing and building fabric.

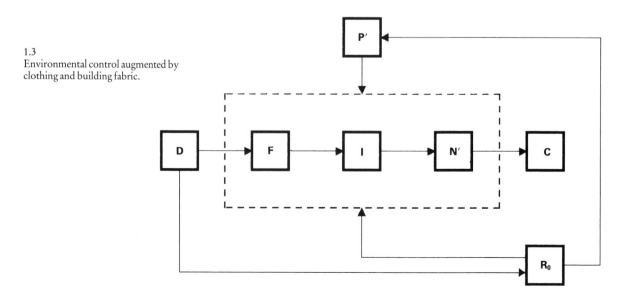

- What is the potential for variation of environmental conditions which is offered by buildings of different types?
- To what extent do the occupants of buildings take active steps to modify the environment, and at what point?
- How wide is the range of conditions which is tolerated?
- Does this 'toleration' demand changes in activity patterns?

The study was based upon specific 'teaching spaces'. All, except one, were distinct classrooms, in five primary schools in Essex, which were made available with generous assistance from the Education and Architect's Departments of Essex County Council. Each was equipped with an extensive monitoring installation to record the major variables of the physical environment – temperatures, lighting levels, etc. – throughout a full annual cycle. These were supplemented by further manual measurements and, most important, by observations of the activities and responses of the occupants.

Clearly, a sample of this size does not produce data which satisfy standard statistical criteria. The project was a pilot study, which aimed to embrace a wide range of environmental variables, rather than isolate a single relationship for study. The results have been described in full elsewhere[6] and only the main conclusions are presented here. Under the heading 'User priorities' it was found that,

Great emphasis was placed by teaching staff on the ability to control the conditions in their own space. The one school in our sample which was mechanically controlled caused the greatest user dissatisfaction . . . User

1.4
Environmental control augmented by plant.

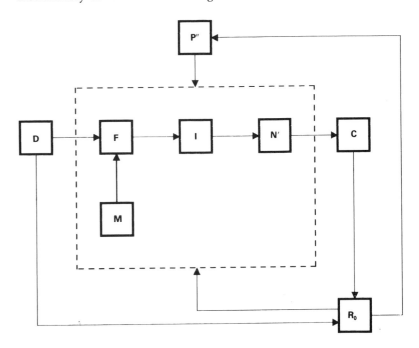

control would seem to be an important source of psychological satisfaction.

User controls available were manipulated in response to external conditions, such as direct sunshine, impinging on the space, and to vary internal conditions to fit teaching requirements . . . A range of conditions was found to be acceptable rather than any exact performance standard. Comfort depended on a complex interaction of air and radiant temperatures, air flow speeds, direct sunshine. The appreciation of these conditions also varied with activity patterns.

Our work shows that, rather than precise fixed standards, a variable environment is preferred. Design standards cannot be set as goals in the design process, but must be set as a range of acceptable levels and interactions.

The study also examined the effect of the design of building elements, 'Performance of the parts'. In this,

. . . the importance of the detailed design of each element became apparent. The design of windows, for example, is a crucially important factor in determining the internal environment . . . In design work it is important to be able to describe this detailed performance . . . for it is at this level that user controls are designed.

From this point the next step was to consider the 'Design of control mechanisms':

Controls which are to be used by a variety of individuals must be comprehensible . . . Immediate response is required by the occupants

1.5
Occupant control augmented by automatic controls.

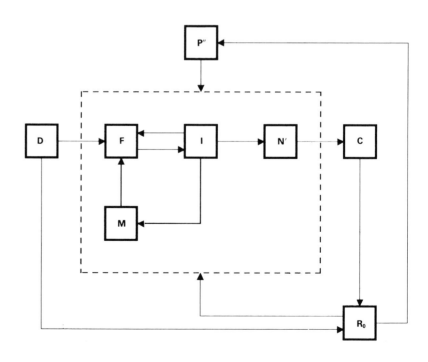

from their action. A response is triggered by unacceptable or inappropriate conditions, which require instant relief . . . The spur to action to rectify discomfort is perhaps more reliable than the memory to return and undo the response when comfort is restored. Thus, especially for energy-consuming mechanisms, a shut-off sensor might have to be combined with the user switch.

The adoption of automatic controls on environmental plant in buildings is often justified by the argument that this ensures efficient use of energy by preventing 'interference' by the occupants. In a building in which mechanical systems are the predominant means of environmental control, exclusive buildings in our definition above, this is almost certainly the case. In a selective building, however, such generalizations can be misleading. This question of the effect of user actions upon 'Energy inputs' was considered in these studies:

We would suggest that by extending user control to achieve a closer meshing of their demands with the environment, considerable energy efficiency can be achieved. Firstly, this process involves detailed examination of the ways in which the external environment impinges on the building and the possible responses of the building to that. Rather than rejecting these influences and seeking to exclude them, certain benefits, such as passive solar heat gains, wind cooling or natural lighting, can be exploited as well as controlled.

Secondly, it is proposed that through the user being able to satisfy his own demands, a closer fit is found between activities and environments. Inputs of energy became more closely allied to needs rather than to maintaining imposed standards. Optimising controls must be developed which balance user demands and forgetfulness with energy criteria; energy should not be spent when not needed when, for example, the windows are open or the room is empty.

A major problem in communicating the results of architectural research to designers lies in the fact that research projects must, almost inevitably, conclude with abstract statements of general principle. Both the theoretical model of the environmental system described here, and the conclusions of the field studies project fall some way short of providing explicit guidance for actual design. In this instance, however, the research workers were given the opportunity to participate in the development of a series of more explicit statements on the architectural implications of their work. In association with the Architect's Department of Hampshire County Council an exploratory study was undertaken.[7] In this the many strands of this research began to come together.

Some studies of the potential of passive solar heating, which is implicit in the general possibilities of selective designs in school buildings, showed that the more dispersed plan forms and elaborate

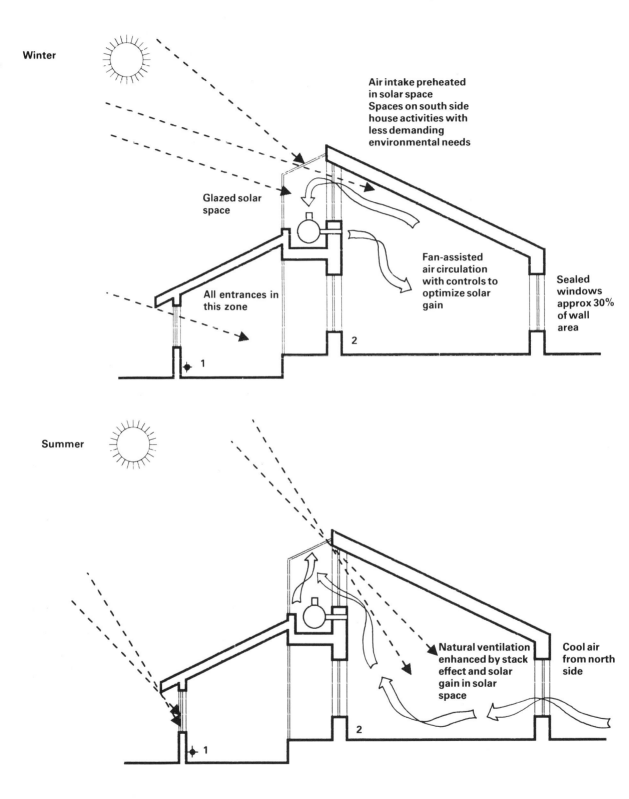

1.6
Cross-section through the teaching wing
of a 'selective mode' building.

1, Ancillary teaching space
2, Classroom space

**Winter**

Air intake preheated
in solar space
Spaces on south side
house activities with
less demanding
environmental needs

Glazed solar
space

Fan-assisted
air circulation
with controls to
optimize solar
gain

Sealed
windows
approx 30%
of wall
area

All entrances in
this zone

1

2

**Summer**

Natural ventilation
enhanced by stack
effect and solar
gain in solar
space

Cool air
from north
side

1

2

**Notes and references**

1
Hawkes, D., 'Environmental models:
past, present and future', in Hawkes,
D., (ed.), *Models and Systems in
Architecture and Building*, Construction
Press, Lancaster, 1975.

2
Musgrove, J., 'Dangers of scientism',
*Architectural Review*, July 1966.

3
Hawkes, D. and Willey, H., 'User
response in the environmental control
system', in *Transactions of the Martin
Centre for Architectural and Urban
Studies*, vol. 2, Woodhead-Faulkner,
Cambridge, 1977.

4
Willey, H., 'The environmental control
system of occupied buildings', in
*Transactions of the Martin Centre for
Architectural and Urban Studies*, vol. 4,
Woodhead-Faulkner, Cambridge, 1980.

5
Baker, N., 'The influence of thermal
comfort and user control on the design
of a passive solar school building:
Locksheath Primary School', *Energy
and Building*, 5 (1982).

6
Haigh, D., 'User response in
environmental control', in Hawkes, D.
and Owers, J., (eds), *The Architecture of
Energy*, Construction Press/Longman,
Harlow, 1982.

7
Haigh, D. and Hawkes, D., report to
Hampshire County Council, 1980.

cross-sections implied by the selective approach could, if properly developed, offer substantial energy savings over conventional designs and, compared favourably with the performance of 'low-energy' versions of the exclusive approach. The formal implications were set out in a proposal for a cross-section through the classroom wing of a primary school. As an essential consequence of the whole approach the difference between winter and summer operation was explicitly drawn (Figure 1.6).

The first point to note about this proposition is the clear distinction made between the major class space, in which it is assumed that the environmental standards will be high and that the full potential of occupant control will be available, and the ancillary areas of practical activities, cloakrooms and so forth, in which the environmental conditions need be less rigorously controlled. This distinction reflects evidence drawn from the survey which showed that a uniformly high standard of environment is not essential throughout a building such as a primary school in which a wide range of activities are accommodated. The application of a similar principle to other building types may produce interesting results.

The configuration of space here ensures that the more sensitive environment of the class space is given a degree of protection from the undesirable effects of a southerly aspect by the ancillary space but that, through the high-level glasshouse, it can derive both a direct and an indirect solar contribution to its heating requirements, and enjoy the qualitative benefits of controlled admission of direct sunlight. The location of all entrances to the building in the ancillary zone also eliminates the problems of environmental disturbance which are often found when class spaces have direct access to the open air.

In operation, the intention is that a building of this type would be 'free-running' in the summer months and for some substantial part of the conventional heating season, whenever climatic conditions are favourable. Only on unfavourable winter days, with no solar contribution, would the mechanical plant be in full use. Even then the control systems would be localized.

These diagrams show only one of the possible architectural arrangements that are implicit in the principles set out by this research. Indeed, one of the attractions of the approach is that, while there are rules which must be respected if the technical and social potential is to be fully realized, these are not architecturally determinate. This should not be surprising when it is recognized that, until the relatively recent dominance of mechanical systems in environmental control, the customary mode of environmental control was akin to the selective. What this work represents is a re-evaluation of long-established principles.

# 2 Building shape and energy use

## Introduction

The question of what shape a building should be is one of the most fundamental issues that confronts an architect. In his discussion of *The Classical Language of Architecture*,[1] Summerson has persuasively demonstrated how the forms of antiquity have served as models for many buildings, during the Renaissance and since, frequently with little or no reference to their original function: the Pantheon form becoming a Christian church, a private house in England and a university library in the USA; and Roman colonnaded circular temples providing the source of reference for objects as diverse as Bramante's Tempietto, Wren's dome at St Paul's Cathedral, Hawksmoor's mausoleum at Castle Howard and James Gibbs' Radcliffe Camera at Oxford.

On the other hand, a historical example of the significance of shape in which functional concerns were important is that of the auditorium of the 'Italian' theatre. Here the predominant influence of good sound and good vision led to the emergence of the 'horseshoe' plan in the seventeenth century and to its survival for more than two centuries as the basis of innumerable designs.

At a more theoretical level it has been suggested that much design depends upon the existence of a 'stereotype', which I defined in 'Types, norms and habit' as 'a generally held notion about the nature of a good solution to any recurrent design problem that frequently inspires the initial design . . .'. This stereotype is invariably defined and recognized as a building shape.

With this demonstrable emphasis upon conceptions of shape, it is not surprising that the emergence of energy conservation as a major issue in design should have led to the question, 'What shape is an energy-conserving building?' And it is equally unsurprising that quick answers were offered. The literature in recent years is full of statements on the following lines:

Buildings should be large rather than small and have circular or square plans, heated buildings should be near cubical in shape, but air-conditioned buildings should be lower, depending on the amount of glazing.[2]

The simplicity of the prescription, allied to the theoretical support it has received, have made this idea of the compact building into a major stereotype for the design of energy-conserving buildings. It represents an approach which undoubtedly has many attractions and much potential for future development, but the answer to our question about the relationship between shape and energy use does not end here. The aim of the discussion that follows is to set out a general framework for energy-conserving design from which we can develop a broader understanding of the issue.

**Approaches to environmental control**

Buildings consume energy principally in the processes of environmental control in mediating between the external climate and the internal environment. If we are to understand how energy may be conserved we should examine the ways in which this control may be achieved. In its most basic sense the problem of environmental control is one of overcoming the extremes and variability of the climate. Olgyay's simple, but elegant, model serves to illustrate the essence of the problem. The first question the designer must answer is, 'How do we define the relationship between the internal and the external environments?'

In considering problems of design in very general terms, the American philosopher of science, Herbert A. Simon, has suggested that there is an underlying symmetry in the problem.

An artifact can be thought of as a meeting point, an "interface" in today's terms, between an "inner" environment and an "outer" environment . . .[3]

In illustrating his proposition, Simon takes the case of clock design in the eighteenth century, particularly the development of the ship's chronometer. Mechanical clocks first appeared on dry land in the fourteenth century, but as navigation developed the benefits of having accurate clocks on board ship became apparent. In 1735 John Harrison of London produced the first successful marine chronometer. The problem was to overcome the effects of the change in the external environment that followed from moving a clock from the mantelpiece to a place on board a storm-tossed ship. Part of the problem was solved by making changes to the internal mechanism, such as the development of compensation to overcome the effects of great changes in temperature, but the real solution lay in the design of the 'interface' between the internal environment of the clock and the external environment on board the ship. This was done by the use of gimbal mounts and a sturdy additional casing.[4]

This example serves as a useful metaphor for a general principle in design. This is that the job of the designer may be greatly simplified if he or she can insulate the primary problem from the effects of external disturbance. This does not, incidentally, mean that the design itself will necessarily be better, but that the act of designing can be made easier.

If we now return to the idea of a compact building as a basis for environmental control, and hence of energy conservation, we can see that it is founded upon exactly the same general principles as the ship's chronometer. In 1967 Hardy and O'Sullivan wrote,

In buildings designed for daylight the demand for heating and cooling is determined mainly by changes in the external environment, which can vary considerably and, therefore, produce widely fluctuating demands for heating and cooling. In buildings designed for PSALI (Permanent Supplementary Artificial Lighting of Interiors) or PAL (Permanent Artificial Lighting), the influence of the external thermal environment can be reduced to such an extent that this becomes a minor factor.[5]

We may label buildings designed in this manner as adopting the 'exclusive mode' in that they use the building envelope to exclude the effects of the external environment upon the internal conditions. But if we consider the approach to environmental control which has predominated historically in temperate climates we see that it has depended upon the selective admission of substantial elements of the external environment into the building. We may thus label this approach the 'selective mode' and can then examine the extent to which it also provides a basis for energy-conserving design.

The essence of these two modes can be further defined by setting up an abstract representation of the 'environmental control system'. Figure 2.1 identifies the principal sources and flows of energy which may be found in a building, the relationships between them, and the mechanisms of control which may be used. By placing boundaries around sections of the diagram we can make clear the difference between the exclusive and selective modes (Figures 2.2 and 2.3). The former depends predominantly, if not completely, upon generated energy and the latter makes use of ambient energy as a major source. The problem of energy-conserving design is thus quite different in each case.

Another distinction which it is valuable to recognize at this stage is the nature of the seasonal energy demands of the two modes (Figure 2.4). In an ideal exclusive design a building would, by definition, consume some generated energy at all times when it was in use, but the peak demand would be small and would not be subject to seasonal variation. A selective building, on the other hand, will consume some generated energy for space heating and lighting during the winter months, but it should be possible for the building fabric alone to provide a comfortable environment for a substantial part of the year – 'free-running' in Humphreys' useful term.[6]

We may thus consider the directions in which development should proceed in order to improve the performance of each type. In the exclusive case the task is to move closer to the ideal straight line of energy use and to lower the level at which it is drawn. The selective case requires efforts to be directed towards the reduction of the peak value of the curve and to shortening its base.

## The relationship between shape and energy use

The exclusive mode, as we have seen, has been the subject of much research and development in practice and its basic qualities are now well understood. The ratio between the surface area and the volume enclosed is the key factor, but this is now viewed in a less dogmatic way than in earlier rule-of-thumb references to the virtues of cube-like buildings. In the paper previously referred to, W.P. Jones discussed the relationship between the glazed area of walls and the form of an air-conditioned (exclusive mode) building.[7] Since glazing is the major route through which the internal environment is disturbed by external factors, principally solar heat gain, the aim is to minimize the consequences of desired window sizes. In simple terms, if the area of glazing in the wall is large a form should be used that trades off total wall area against roof area, in other words a low–deep form. If the glazed area is reduced, the ratio of wall area to roof area can be increased and the form tends towards a cube (Figure 2.5).

An important theoretical concept used in the design of an exclusive mode building is the 'thermal balance point'. A relationship is established between the form and properties of the building envelope and the internal sources of energy in the building (Figure 2.6). By careful control of the variables it is possible to produce a design in which the balance temperature is low enough to eliminate the need for a heating system. In the use of this technique there may be a temptation to aim for a very low balance point on the assumption that this equates with low energy use. Mitchell cites examples of buildings in Britain with balance points of $-5.5°C$ and $-1.0°C$.[8] But a consequence of setting a very low balance point in a temperate climate is a corresponding increase in the cooling requirement of the building and, frequently, an embarrassment of recovered heat for much of the year.

It would be worthwhile examining the effects of setting the balance point in the range of, say, $4°C–8°C$ and accepting the need to use a modest back-up heating system on the relatively small number of very cold winter days. This energy use would be offset by the reduction in the amount of recovered heat which is then thrown away. If the manipulation of the balance point was achieved

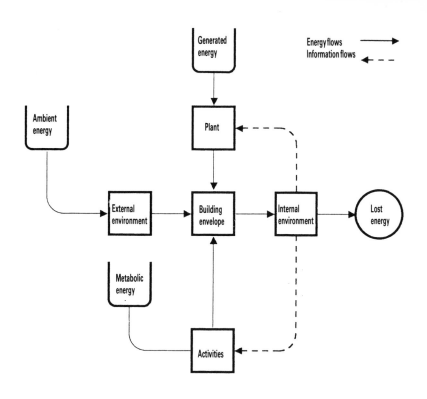

2.1
The environmental control system.

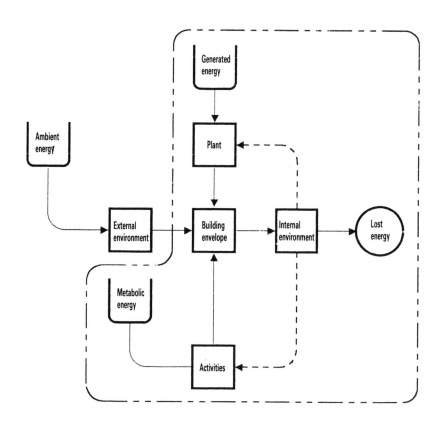

2.2
The 'exclusive mode' subsystem.

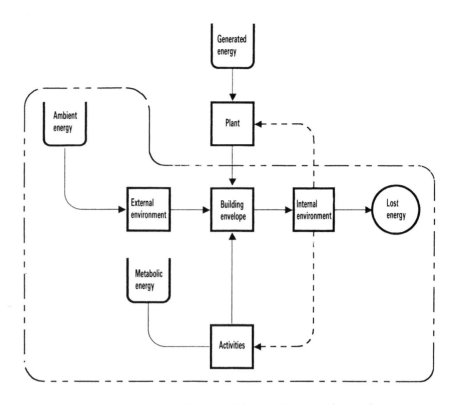

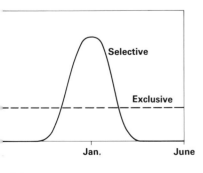

by varying the form of the building, adjusting the surface area to volume ratio, we could then see exclusive mode buildings begin to break away from the formal straight-jacket of compact plan orthodoxy without sacrificing their inherent attractions of predictable performance and a high level of environmental control for a relatively modest capital expenditure.

As mentioned previously, the selective mode is the traditional approach to environmental control in temperate climates. Its relative lack of influence upon the initial phase of energy-conserving design in the non-domestic field was probably due to historical accident. In the early 1970s much practice was dominated by the attractions of air conditioning and other mechanical systems in the design of large buildings. There was also a good deal of conspicuous environmental failure in buildings that combined traditional modes of environmental control with new methods of construction such as curtain-walling. Within an evolutionary view of design, such as is implied by the argument about the role of the stereotype, it was almost inevitable that the first moves in the development of 'low-energy' buildings would continue along the established path. But, as any thorough-going Darwinian would point out, it was equally likely that a diversification of approach would eventually occur and that this would make some reference to earlier precedents.

We have seen that the selective approach is characterized by its use of ambient energy and its 'free-running' capability in the

41 | Building shape and energy use

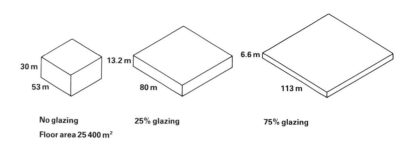

30 m
13.2 m
6.6 m
53 m
80 m
113 m

No glazing
25% glazing
75% glazing

Floor area 25 400 m²

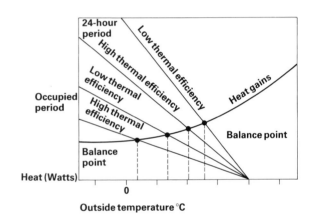

24-hour
period
Low thermal efficiency
High thermal efficiency
Low thermal efficiency
Occupied period
Low thermal efficiency
High thermal efficiency
Heat gains
Balance point
High thermal efficiency
Balance point
Heat (Watts)
0
Outside temperature °C

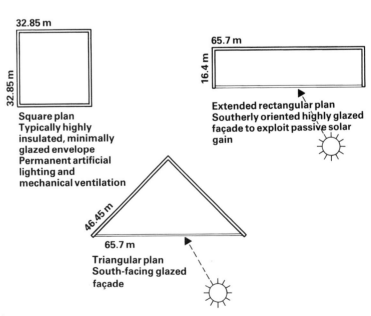

32.85 m

32.85 m

Square plan
Typically highly
insulated, minimally
glazed envelope
Permanent artificial
lighting and
mechanical ventilation

65.7 m

16.4 m

Extended rectangular plan
Southerly oriented highly glazed
façade to exploit passive solar
gain

46.45 m

65.7 m

Triangular plan
South-facing glazed
façade

42 | The Environmental Tradition

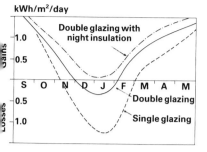

2.8
Window energy balance.

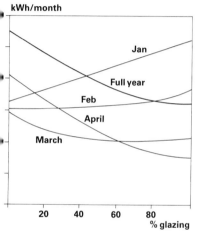

2.9
Variation of heating demand with
percentage of south-facing glazing.

summer months in a temperate climate. The development of
selective, energy-conserving designs thus depends upon the cost-
effective exploitation of ambient energy without incurring any
penalty in terms of environmental discomfort.

In non-domestic buildings, 'ambient energy' means heat and
light. A cornerstone of exclusive theory is that windows are a major
source of disturbance of the internal environment and that their size
should, therefore, be kept within strict bounds. The logic of this
argument depends upon the reduction of summer cooling loads
leading to economies in the use of air conditioning. The selective,
free-running building is, by definition, one in which summertime
overheating is avoided by means that do not consume energy, in
which solar gain is regarded as a desirable input in the heating
season and in which natural lighting is seen as a major component
of the environment. The discussion of the relationship between
shape and energy use thus begins from a completely different
standpoint.

The need to achieve effective penetration of natural light into a
selective building directly bears upon plan form and cross-section,
and the exploitation of solar heat makes orientation of fundamental
importance. The consequences of these factors can be indicated, if
not exhausted, by making reference to a simple exploratory study
in which alternative arrangements of a fixed amount of floor space
were compared (Figure 2.7). The first form is a single-storey square
in which it is assumed that the principles of exclusive design are
applied. In the two other forms, one a rectangle, the other
triangular, we assume that a major façade faces south and that
advantageous solar gain is admitted through it.

With careful design a south-facing façade can receive a sufficient
amount of passive solar gain to offset the heat that it will lose due to
conduction during the winter months (Figures 2.8 and 2.9). In a
building in which, as is the case for most non-domestic types,
occupancy is restricted to the 'working day', the coincidence of
useful passive solar gain and use is particularly valuable. Assuming
that the south façade has an effective U-value of **zero** W/m²/°C we
can make a simple comparison between the fabric heat loss in each
of the three forms:

| Form | Heat-loss coefficient (W/°C/m²) |
| --- | --- |
| 1. Square plan | 0.81 |
| 2. Rectangle – 4 : 1 | 0.64 |
| 3. Triangle | 0.63 |

These calculations assume that walls and roofs in all cases have a
U-value of 0.5 W/m²/°C, that windows other than those in the
south façades of Forms 2 and 3 have a U-value of 3.0 W/m²/°C
(double glazing). The square plan is taken to have 15% of its wall

area glazed and the non-southerly walls of Forms 2 and 3 have 30% glazing. Ventilation loss is ignored in all cases. More detailed analysis on the same assumptions using the standard procedure for energy-consumption calculations in educational buildings shows that, when primary energy-consumption factors are taken into account, these two selective forms easily met official design standards.

These simple diagrams are, of course, far removed from real buildings, but they do establish a basic measure of the potential of the selective approach. Detailed analysis shows that, even with the increase in external surface area over the theoretical cases, this design offers a comparable performance and competes with that offered by exclusive designs.

The use of the selective mode is particularly well suited to school buildings, but its characteristics are equally appropriate for many other building types. If I may refer to an earlier line of thought,[9] the land-use potential of the court form, which lends itself to selective control, has been amply demonstrated (Figure 2.10).

It is possible to summarize the general characteristics of buildings designed in each mode of environmental control (Table 2.1).

Table 2.1  General characteristics of exclusive and selective mode buildings

| Exclusive mode | Selective mode |
| --- | --- |
| *Environment* is automatically controlled and is predominantly artificial | *Environment* is controlled by a combination of automatic and manual means and is a variable mixture of natural and artificial. |
| *Shape* is compact, seeking to minimize the interaction between exterior and interior environments. | *Shape* is dispersed, seeking to maximize the use of ambient energy. |
| *Orientation* is relatively unimportant. | *Orientation* is a crucial factor. |
| *Windows* are generally restricted in size. | *Windows* are large on southerly façades and restricted to the north. Solar controls are required to avoid summer overheating. |
| *Energy* is primarily from generated sources and is used throughout the year in a relatively constant quantity. | *Energy* is a combination of ambient and generated. The use is variable throughout the year with a peak in the winter and 'free-running' in the summer. |

## Conclusion

This discussion began by arguing that successful design in architecture frequently rests upon the establishment at the outset of an

2.10
Land use and built form – pavilions and courtyards compared.

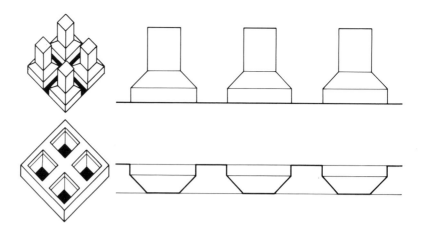

## Notes and references

1
Summerson, J., *The Classical Language of Architecture*, Revised edition, Thames & Hudson, London, 1980.

2
Jones, W.P., 'Built form and energy needs', in Sherratt, A.F.C., (ed.), *Energy Conservation and Energy Management in Buildings*, Applied Science, London, 1976.

3
Simon, H.A., 'Understanding the material and artificial worlds, in *The Sciences of the Artificial*, MIT Press, Cambridge, Mass., 1969.

4
Brunton, E., *Clocks and Watches, 1400–1900*, Arthur Baker, London, 1967.

5
Hardy, A. and O'Sullivan, P., *Insolation and Fenestration*, Oriel Press, Newcastle, 1967.

6
Humphreys, M.A., 'Outdoor temperatures and comfort indoors', Building Research Establishment, Garston, Current Paper 53/78, 1978.

7
Jones, W.P., *op. cit.*

8
Mitchell, H.G., 'Heat recovery in buildings', in *The Efficient Use of Electricity in Buildings*, The Electricity Council, London, 1975.

9
Martin, L. and March, L., 'Built form and land use', *Cambridge Research*, April 1966.

appropriate building shape. By developing a distinction between two basic modes of environmental control I have tried to show that the relationship between shape and energy use is not formally deterministic. But there are principles that can be made explicit which define the limits of shape for energy-conserving designs. There may be further developments along the path of exclusive control or may equally be investigations into the emerging, or re-emerging, potential of the selective mode of environmental control. I cannot resist, even in my conclusion, suggesting that there may be other possibilities that fall outside my categorization and which combine elements of the two modes in the form of hybrids! Why, for example, shouldn't the environment in exclusive buildings be sustained, in part at least, by ambient energy sources collected on their relatively windowless façades?

It is clear that energy-conserving design does not permit merely gratuitous form-making because there are identifiable constraints upon the designer which cannot be ignored. It is equally clear that certain forms which have met past needs are no longer acceptable. But it is now possible to show that the term 'low-energy building' allows many possibilities of shape. Among these are established types of demonstrated utility, a whole range of new possibilities and re-evaluations of old types which have fallen from favour. All of these are directly provoked by asking the question, 'What shape is a low-energy building?'

# 3  Types, norms and habit in environmental design

The process of architectural design is essentially some way of proceeding from statements of design objectives to a solution which is judged to be 'satisfactory'. Leaving aside the problems of expressing design objectives and measuring 'satisfactoriness', consider for a moment the nature of the process itself. Among the many models of the process of design that have been proposed there recurs a scheme in which some idea about a probable solution, a hypothesis, is subjected to a process of analysis in which its measurable performance is compared against the stated objectives. In most of these schemes the model iterates through a progressive process of modification of the initial hypothesis, followed by retesting, until a solution is found which is close to the defined goals. Even those designers who have reservations about the value of an explicit design methodology would very probably, if pressed, acknowledge that their approach to the design of buildings does contain at some stage the essence of this process. The interaction which occurs between mind, eye, pencil and the proverbial back-of-the-envelope can be viewed in this way.

The differences between the 'rationalists' and 'mystics' of architecture could be said to be, in this respect at least, primarily semantic and are thus irrelevant to our discussion. However, what they have in common is our concern: namely the need to arrive at the first hypothesis in some way or another. At their extremes the opposing schools would claim that this is either arrived at by rational analysis of the problem in all its respects or that it is the product of some private alchemy. It can be doubted if either of these views is realistic. More probably, the starting point for most building design is the 'stereotype' solution.

In order to enlarge upon this view, the term stereotype must be clarified. In this context, it is simply a generally held notion about the nature of a good solution to any recurrent building design problem that frequently inspires the initial design hypothesis. In design circles the term stereotype often has pejorative overtones, but it can, and frequently does, play a creative role by allowing the designer to begin the cycle of analysis and revision from a reasonably confident position.

If the validity of this view of the design activity is accepted, it follows that the discussion can generalize about the nature and performance of built forms by examining their stereotypes. This offers the opportunity to make broad judgements which avoid the danger of being distracted by the ingenuity of the solution of particular problems, of the kind which occur in most building designs. It also allows a review of the present position against a background of the attitudes and predilections of the past. By giving this longer perspective it is possible that patterns may emerge which are obscured at close range and that these patterns may suggest new directions for the future.

As an illustration of this principle the stereotype of the British form of the office building in the first part of the twentieth century has been reviewed. This serves to illustrate that a dynamic relationship exists between the stereotype and the specific design, but, and this is perhaps of greater significance, also reveals trends in the nature of the object which raise important questions about current attitudes to environmental comfort and control.

**An evolutionary tale**

During the early part of the twentieth century the central urban office building in Britain was an object between five and seven storeys in height with either banking or shop space at the ground floor and daylit office space above. Most buildings were relatively small and shared party walls with their neighbours. Construction was usually steel frame with masonry cladding. Environmental control was by means of natural ventilation, steam or hot-water central heating and artificial lighting by electricity was regarded as very much a night-time substitute for daylight (Figure 3.1).

A significant landmark in the development of the office building was the London Passenger Transport Board Building in Westminster of 1929, designed by by Charles Holden. This proposed the idea of 'putting the lightwells on the outside' by adopting a cruciform plan for the main office floors and thus maximizing the daylight the building received by increasing the distance between itself and neighbouring buildings and by eliminating the lightwell. In terms of construction and equipment there is little difference between this stereotype and its predecessor (Figure. 3.2).

The increasing importance of daylighting and sunlighting considerations in town planning practice and legislation led to further developments after the 1939–45 war. The first of these was the notion of encouraging the comprehensive redevelopment of large central area sites of around two acres on the lines proposed in the 'Final Report on the Reconstruction of the City of London'.[1] The emphasis was still on natural lighting with the move towards opening up the urban fabric, which the London Transport building

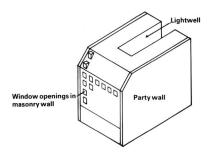

3.1
Stereotype 1, *c.* 1900: London Building Acts, lightwell form.

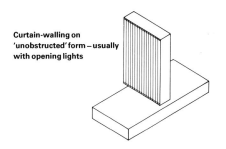

3.4
Stereotype 4, *c.* 1955: slab-on-podium.

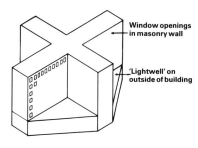

3.2
Stereotype 2, *c.* 1930: 'lightwells on the outside'.

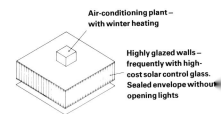

3.5
Stereotype 5, *c.* 1970: deep-plan, air-conditioned.

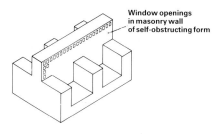

3.3
Stereotype 3, *c.* 1945: postwar daylighting standards.

3.6
Stereotype 6, *c.* 1975: Integrated Environmental Design (IED).

symbolized, now supported by a proposed legislative framework. Once again, the developments in construction and services were not significant. A maximum height of ten storeys was considered to be adequate for all requirements. This stereotype should be familiar to students of the architecture of the postwar years (Figure 3.3).

The influence of daylighting controls as they were eventually taken into planning practice[2] along with inspiration from the other side of the Atlantic, specifically Skidmore, Owings & Merrill's Lever House in New York of 1952, led directly to our next stereotype, the slab-on-podium form of the latter half of the 1950s (Figure 3.4). In Britain this remained a partitioned, daylit form, unlike its American precedents. Simultaneous with the emergence of this form there occurred the first major innovation in constructional technology. This was the acceptance into common practice of the curtain-walling idea. This transformed the outer skin of the building from a heavyweight membrane with 'punched' apertures into a transparent film wrapped around the structural form, with any opaque areas being lightweight infill panels.

This stereotype is the central point of this story because its shortcomings drew attention to problems of environmental control in office buildings for the first time. The conjunction of large areas of glazing, lightweight structures, hitherto unheard-of building heights, a form which maximized the surface area of the enclosure, and the effects of the daylighting legislation which reduced the amount of mutual protection from direct sunlight which is enjoyed by closely packed buildings, all conspired to produce, apparently overnight, severe solar heat-gain problems. These often produced intolerable environmental conditions and much effort has been dedicated to the solution of the 'problem' ever since. This is reflected in the next stages in the evolution of the type.

In response to the environmental shortcomings of the early slab-on-podium buildings, attention was drawn to the previously little-explored attractions of air conditioning. This was quickly followed by a growing interest in deeper plans with a high degree of artificial control over the total environment. The organizational properties of the form were realized with the coming of the open-plan office. On large sites the form was frequently a scaled-up version of the slab-on-podium, but on smaller sites a lower, squatter form emerged (Figure 3.5). Full air conditioning was used, heating in winter and cooling in summer. Along with open-planning came increases in illumination levels to provide a bright environment in deep spaces and attention was drawn to new problems of noise control in large spaces.

This form led to high running costs for the environmental control systems, and by implication high energy consumption, at least by comparison with those of the less sophisticated earlier forms. Further refinement followed until the concept of 'thermal

49 | Types, norms and habit in environmental design

balance' emerged, in which an optimum relationship is sought between levels of environmental provision and the means by which they are achieved and maintained (Figure 3.6).

The first point to note about this building form is that the environment within it is specified with great precision, which is as necessary for the functioning of the systems within it as it is for the comfort of the people who work in it. Illumination levels are specified that maximize 'visual performance' and also demand a large number of light fittings to be installed. The heat from these is then utilized to provide the bulk, if not all, of the heating input into the building during the winter. Temperatures are controlled within fine limits and the ventilation rate selected is a nice compromise between the needs of the occupants for the renewal of the air which they breathe and the need economically to maintain the thermal balance of the building. The fact that the exclusion of external noise is recognized as a problem in central urban areas is exploited to support a decision to reduce the size of the windows and to seal them. This conveniently assists the thermal balance by reducing the effects of solar heat and simultaneously requiring the use of artificial lighting. The whole emphasis is upon control – not in the sense of each occupant having the opportunity to determine his or her own environment, except perhaps for limited options like the freedom to switch a desk lamp on or off, but in the maintenance of an environment between narrow limits.

From this brief history a number of observations can be made. In the first place it can be seen how the elements of the 'hardware' of the building, its fabric and its systems, have, from an environmental control point of view, become progressively more integrated. This is not merely in the usual sense of achieving a tidy arrangement of the services, but also in the way in which they have become operationally interdependent. The second observation is about the 'software' of environmental control, namely the goals which are set.

At the beginning of the evolutionary tale, building science was in its infancy and the quantitative expression of design objectives was barely practised. As a direct consequence, of course, quantitative procedures in environmental design were almost unheard of. During the intervening years building science has come of age and has had a profound influence upon the way goals are stated and achieved, i.e. upon the process of design itself. Along with the parallel and frequently related developments in the technologies of construction and equipment of buildings, this growth in skills of specification and prediction has been a fundamental force in the determination of the nature of the built form. The comparison between the first and last of our stereotypes is clear evidence of how far the built form has evolved.

The first stereotype was recognizably an office building, but its main spatial elements were similar to those encountered in other building types of the period. These elements were complete 'environmental systems', which had evolved slowly by a kind of architectural natural selection. In them all, the critical relationships between plan form, floor-to-ceiling height, the size of window openings, the heating system and ideas about what represented environmental comfort were resolved in a relaxed and flexible manner. The stereotype, because of its looseness, did not intimidate designers, but gave them a starting point and permitted, even invited, further development and exploration in the design process.

The last stereotype in the sequence is very different. It is highly determined and its internal logic can be demonstrated with great precision by a wealth of quantitative evidence. In the introductory discussion of the role of the stereotype in the process of design, it was suggested that it represents the starting point for creative design. If it becomes too highly determined it can no longer fulfil this role. This is particularly the case where its justification is founded upon a 'scientific' basis which is largely inaccessible to the majority of designers. In view of this, the stereotype ought to be examined very closely. This examination may reveal its validity as a general solution to the problem of accommodating office workers. The view of building design that underlies and informs much of our activity in building science may also be examined.

## Environmental comfort and determinism

The first question to raise about the deep-plan stereotype is the desirability of levels of provision and control from the point of view of the occupants of a building. It can be shown that human beings can be comfortable over a wide range of conditions. It can be argued that some temporal variation in conditions is desirable. These considerations force an examination of what is really meant by environmental comfort within buildings and the means by which it can be provided.

To amplify this argument let us look at some of the established relationships between components of the environment and the physiology of comfort. Thermal comfort is a complex phenomenon. In the simplest terms human beings are comfortable when the heat produced by the formal functioning of the body is lost at a rate that is equal to its production. The three mechanisms of heat loss are evaporation, radiation and convection (Figure 3.7).

There are a number of more complex expressions of comfort in these circumstances. These allow an exploration of the effects of parameters other than air temperature alone. A precise definition of thermal comfort can then be constructed to show acceptable relationships between air and mean radiant temperatures, between air speed and the temperature of the air, and, finally, to include the

3.7
Metabolism and body loss *v.*
temperature (after Billington, 1967).

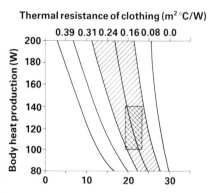

Figure 3.7 graph

3.8
Relationship between temperature,
activity and clothing.

properties of various types of clothing which have, of course, highly local effects upon comfort (Figure 3.8). The effect of relative humidity upon perceived comfort is insignificant provided it is within the range 30 to 70%.

The direct implication of all of this is to show that thermal comfort can be achieved by many combinations of values of parameters of the environment, and that, even in terms of a composite index such as the resultant temperature, there exists a relatively widely defined comfort zone.

This has, or should have, profound implications for the form, detailed design and equipment of buildings. The first thing to stress is that because of the variety of means of providing thermal comfort the range of potential design solutions is wide not narrow. Having said this, what it can mean in architectural terms can be shown by simple example.

On a hot summer day it should be possible to achieve extremely acceptable conditions for some office organizations in a shallow-plan building of relatively heavy construction and with natural ventilation. If the situation is analysed in simple terms, the air temperature in the building is about the same as the outdoor air temperature, but the mean radiant temperature of the internal surfaces is low because of the high thermal capacity of the building. If a high proportion of the glazed area is openable the problem of solar heat gain can be virtually eliminated and simple roller blinds can cope easily with the problem of direct solar radiation falling upon the occupants. The flow of air through the building means that relatively high air temperatures will be acceptable. The shallow plan ensures that natural lighting is adequate for most jobs, eliminating the need for artificial sources with their consequent heat input.

It is interesting to note the internal logic of this building form which, in its own terms, is as consistent as that of the thermal balance building in the deep-plan stereotype. The difference between the two 'systems' is that one is universal while the other only works if a host of factors fall within certain bounds. To put this another way, one is sensitive to its local environment to the extent that its success depends upon the existence and maintenance of certain conditions; the other can be made to work in a variety of circumstances.

Turning now to visual comfort, the first point to make is that the human eye is extremely adaptable. It is possible to read newsprint by moonlight where the illumination level is a mere 0.5 lux and by the outdoor illumination on a sunny day where the level may be in the order of 25 000 lux. As in the case of the basic definition of thermal comfort, the comfort zone is normally narrowed for the purposes of building design. The usual method is to establish some correlation between levels of illumination and visual acuity.

The main implication of this is that, although it can be shown that visual acuity increases with increase in illumination level, it does so in a logarithmic relationship so that a doubling of performance requires a tenfold increase in the lighting level. In practice this means that after the minimum acceptable level of illumination for a particular task has been established the benefits of any increase must be traded off against all the other consequences. The balance between natural and artificial lighting is one instance and, if the emphasis is upon artificial lighting, the effects of increasing levels upon capital and running costs, and the problems and costs of handling or exploiting the heat produced, should be evaluated.

It is clear that acoustical design in office buildings is a matter of ensuring that noise levels within them do not inconvenience desired communication while ensuring, with or without the help of partitions or screens, that privacy can be found when required. This suggests that the exclusion of traffic noise as a general design objective is irrelevant. There are some conceivable situations in which intelligent planning of a building, combined with careful design of its envelope, could make use of the external noise in the service of the internal acoustical needs. Other building briefs on a similar site might make exclusion essential, and there are yet other combinations of brief and location in which the 'manufacture' of masking noise is necessary if the building is to work satisfactorily.

The point of this discussion is to stress the indeterminacy of the findings of research into human environmental comfort in buildings. On this evidence it is curious that the effects and emphasis of much work in building science have been deterministic.

The prime purposes of this essay are to question an orthodoxy and to set forth an outline of some problems that arise when the stereotype becomes too precisely defined. The error lies in the too ready acceptance of a grossly oversimplified model of the process of design in architecture. This model is implicit in the proposition that *form follows function*, which is laden with deterministic implications. The relationship has become not only an observation that

53 | Types, norms and habit in environmental design

can be made about the links between problem and solution, but is also frequently interpreted literally as a scheme for the process by which the problem is transformed into the solution.

With the growth of the quantitative expression of design objectives, it was clearly necessary to develop means by which the performance of designs could be checked. Consequently, the production of design aids of one kind or another has been a major concern of building research.[3] These techniques frequently represent a compromise between accuracy and applicability and, as such, they sometimes embody simplified views of complex phenomena.

One possible simplification lies in the specification of the design goals themselves and this is particularly the case in respect of most of the measures of environmental comfort. For example, it is much simpler to calculate the heat input required to maintain a building at a specified air temperature under hypothetically stable external conditions than to make a detailed assessment of the total thermal environment as expressed by, say, the more complex equivalent temperature, taking into account the dynamic effects of the ever-changing external climate, the activities of the occupants and the inputs of the control systems.

After the encouraging success achieved in quantifying design goals and in the development of design aids, it is understandable that the dream of the optimum design attracted attention. But it is here, it could be argued, that the application of quantitative methods in architectural design went astray. This seductive prospect could be said to have clouded its enthusiasts' judgement and to have led them to forget or fail to observe the true nature of the process of design. Their model of the design process fails on the most fundamental criterion, namely, that it must be an accurate representation of at least some part of the reality to which it relates. A model that fails here, however elegant and internally logical it appears to be, is bound to deceive its user. The reality of architectural design is extremely complex and, while recognition of this fact should not be a deterrent from making attempts to understand it, it does demand caution against falling into the trap of adopting oversimplifications.

In environmental design, the model's crucial failing is its inability to acknowledge that the goal of 'comfort' can be achieved in many ways, both in terms of the values attached to the design parameters and in terms of the architectural and technological means by which they are provided. The evidence offered by this study of the stereotype shows a worrying trend towards an inflexibility of form which is justified only by a closed logic and ignores some of the real needs of people in the built environment.

## Conclusion

It is now necessary to draw together the threads of the argument and to try to propose a basis for design that acknowledges the role of the stereotype and that, at the same time, avoids the dangers which arise when a particular stage in its development is too highly determined.

The answer appears to lie in the realization that the latest stereotype does not supersede all others. There is, in fact, a store of accumulated experience which contains all previous solutions and which will be enlarged in the future with the addition of new examples informed by changing building technology, organizational ideas and physical, social and cultural contexts. This view demands a return to earlier stereotypes to see what they offer as potential solutions to present-day problems and to see what they might offer when modified to exploit developments in technology that have occurred since their day. A healthy situation would be one in which solutions with a high dependence on mechanical systems could coexist with others which achieved their goals by simpler means. There are certainly many situations where the thinking behind the thermal balance stereotype would be appropriate, even necessary, in order to provide an environment of the quality which is often demanded today, but there are other instances where a significantly different approach would be acceptable and appropriate.

The search should be for the most appropriate solution to each particular set of problems. Within the hypothetico-analytical scheme of design, the first step would be to examine the store of stereotypes rather than simply to accept a single current notion about the nature of the solution. A process of evaluation would suggest the area in which the solution lay and the design would proceed from this. The result would be a richness of solutions inspired by the particular nature of each problem and the achievement of building science would find its true place within a proper understanding of the nature of design.

## Notes and references

1
Holden, C.H. and Holford, W.G., *A new plan for the City of London*, The Architectural Press, London, 1947.

2
Allen, W. and Crompton, D., 'A form of control of building development in terms of daylighting', *RIBA Journal*, August, 1947.

3
Hawkes, D., 'Environmental models: past, present and future' in Hawkes, D. (Ed.), *Models and Systems in Architecture and Building*, Construction Press, Lancaster, 1975.

# Precedent and theory in the design of auditoria

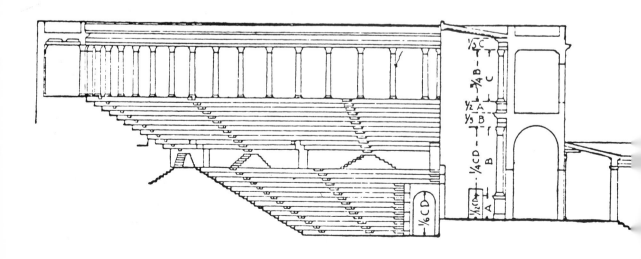

# Introduction

This essay sets out to review the historical development of the theory and practice of auditorium design and, from this, to point to a fundamental distinction which exists between the use of precedent and of explanatory theory in the design of this building type, and, indeed, of all complex buildings.

From the outset auditorium form was essentially the product of the designer's interpretation of the requirements for 'good sound' and 'good vision'. The forms of Greek and Roman theatres, as described by Vitruvius (Figure 4.1), are explicitly related to ancient acoustic theory:

> voice is a flowing breath of air, perceptible to the hearing by contact. It moves in an endless number of circular rounds . . . Hence the ancient architects, following in the footsteps of nature, perfected the descending rows of seats in theatres from their investigations of the ascending voice . . .[1]

The most striking facts that emerge from a review of auditorium design since Vitruvius are the powerful influence of precedent upon design and that throughout this lengthy history there have been only a few basic auditorium forms. The reason for this is almost certainly a reflection of the complexity of the relationships between form and performance, particularly in acoustics, and the inability, until quite recently, of theory to do much more than explain the success of certain forms and the failure of others.

When the theatre came indoors in the Renaissance the principal reference was, at first, not surprisingly, to the designs of antiquity. Andrea Palladio's Teatro Olimpico at Vicenza of *c.* 1550 (Figure 4.2) clearly reveals its debt to Vitruvius, as does Vincenzo Scamozzi's design for the theatre at Sabbioneta of 1588 (Figure 4.3). This precedent also determined the arrangement of the auditorium in Gianbattista Aleotti's Teatro Farnese at Parma completed in 1628. Here, however, probably for the first time a proscenium arch was introduced, which allowed movable scenery to be used. The ancient precedent was adopted so literally in these designs that the colonnade at the rear of the auditorium was retained, even though its original purpose of providing shelter for the audience in the event of sudden showers was clearly redundant.

As theatre-going became a public activity, the model underwent a series of transformations in order to accommodate larger audiences and to reflect the social order of the community by clear segregation. Carlo Fontana's Teatro Tor di Nona at Rome, dated 1671, represents a significant point in this transformation (Figure 4.4) and, with its horseshoe-shaped tiers of boxes rising above the stalls and pit, established a precedent for theatre design which was to dominate practice for more than two centuries. There were,

4.1
Roman theatre, after Vitruvius.

4.2
Andrea Palladio, Teatro Olimpico,
Vicenza, *c.* 1550.

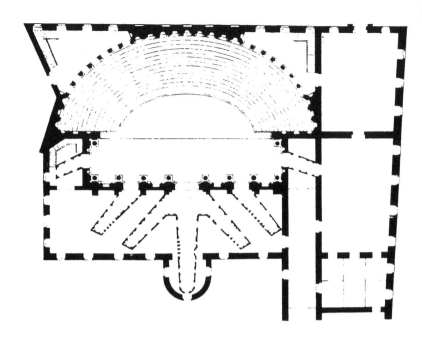

4.3
Vincenzo Scamozzi, theatre at
Sabbioneta, 1588.

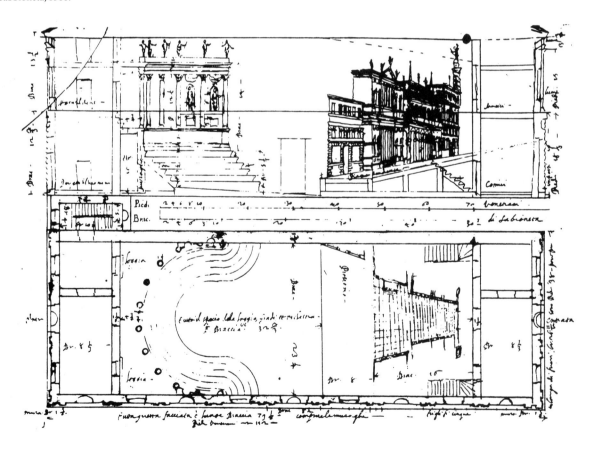

clearly, deviations in detail from the precedent in response to local conditions, particularly of size and social organization, and also to developments in the style and scale of productions, particularly to accommodate the needs of opera which had emerged as a distinct dramatic form at the beginning of the seventeenth century. Nonetheless, the great majority of theatres built for opera in Europe, and later in the USA, were based on this 'standard' arrangement as the examples in Figure 4.5 help to demonstrate.

The dominance of this model forces us to ask why it was so attractive. The answer must be that it offered a satisfactory solution to the problem of theatre design, and that the problem itself did not change significantly during this period. In these circumstances there would be little incentive to experiment. We should not ignore, however, the fact that, in other respects, architectural theory underwent wide-ranging transformations in this period. In terms of conventional stylistic classification, these buildings stretch from the high Renaissance, through mannerism, the baroque and rococo up to the classical revival of the nineteenth century. As Rudolf Wittkower has shown, humanity's conception of its own place and, as a consequence, the basis of architectural theory, changed fundamentally during these two centuries.

Within the terms of a new conception of the world the whole structure of classical aesthetics was systematically broken up, and in this process man's vision underwent a decisive change.[2]

In the face of these events it is perhaps surprising that the standard form of auditorium survived so long, in spite of its obvious utility. What we should recognize here is that the changes that were taking place represented the breakdown of the all-embracing vision of the Renaissance world into an essentially 'atomistic' view of nature, art and particularly science. To quote Wittkower again,

With the rise of the new science the synthesis which had held microcosm and macrocosm together, that all-pervading order and harmony in which thinkers had believed from Pythagoras' day to the 16th and 17th centuries began to disintegrate.

Given then that architectural form need no longer obey comprehensive rules of proportion and relationship, architects pursued the dictates of current theory in the design of theatre buildings, but at the same time they retained the successful empirically derived model for the most difficult space of all, the auditorium. If we recognize that the ancient laws of acoustics had little relevance to the problem of the indoor theatre and to the needs of the new dramatic forms, and that the new sciences had not yet produced a reliable theoretical basis for this aspect of design, the attractions of a workable model become very clear. In the design of the Paris

4.5
The 'horse-shoe' plan: a) Teatro Regio,
Turin; b) Théâtre de Lyon; c) Royal
Opera House, London.

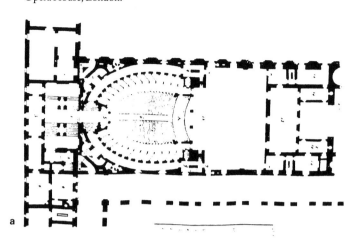

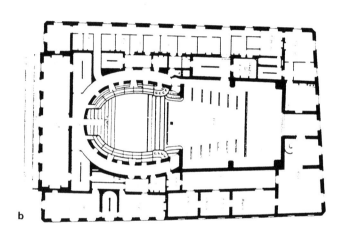

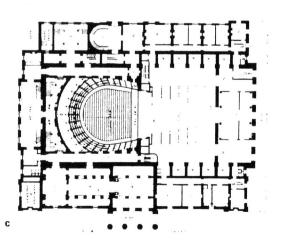

4.4
Carlo Fontana, Teatro Tor di Nona,
Rome, 1671.

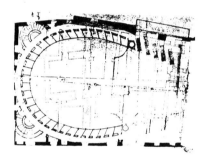

Opera, 1861–75, Charles Garnier claimed to have carried out a study of acoustics but was, in the end, defeated by what he called 'this bizarre science'. As the plan (Figure 4.6) shows he was, however, able to rely on the safe precedent of the standard auditorium form, modelled in this case specifically on Victor Louis' design at the Grand Theatre, Bordeaux, 1780, the success of the design even at this late stage demonstrating the value of the model.

The power of this precedent in auditorium design was challenged in a number of ways during the nineteenth century, perhaps most significantly by the alliance between Ludwig II of Bavaria, Richard Wagner and Gottfried Semper. Wagner's original conception of the nature of orchestral sound and his insistence upon better sightlines than the Italian horseshoe plan allowed, and Semper's neoclassicism, both aided by royal enthusiasm, converged to produce a design that was quite unlike any theatre built for over two centuries. Even here, however, there was very little fundamental innovation, apart from details such as Wagner's sunken orchestra pit, since the reference to the Vitruvian/Palladian form is quite clear, even to the rear colonnade. This project for Munich, 1865–66, was never built, but Wagner retained its main features in the Bayreuth Festspielhaus executed by Otto Brückwald and opened in 1876 (Figure 4.7). It is interesting to note that when Semper designed the new Hoftheater in Dresden, following the fire of 1871, he reverted to the horseshoe auditorium, even though the exterior form of the building, with its implication of an amphitheatre, owed much to the Wagner project.

The history of the concert hall is very different since the idea of secular public performance was a relatively late development in music. In the nineteenth century, however, when there was a spate of concert hall construction, a powerful precedent emerged which provided a basis for successful design. This was the rectangular 'shoebox' hall with perhaps one, or exceptionally, two shallow balconies. The major halls in Vienna, 1870; Basel, 1876; Glasgow, 1877; Leipzig, 1886; Amsterdam, 1888; and Boston, 1900, all conform to this model (Figure 4.8).

## The role of scientific theory

At the end of the nineteenth century, therefore, most buildings for opera and concerts owed their basic auditorium form to well-established precedents. It appeared that if these models were respected, they offered a designer a reasonable prospect of success, particularly since the available 'theoretical' guidance was demonstrably contradictory and unreliable.

It was into this situation that W.C. Sabine came at the very end of the century and carried out the research work that laid the foundations of modern architectural acoustics.[3] His insight into the relationship between a physical measure of sound, reverberation time, and subjective perceptions of sound quality, and the crucial link between this measure and architecturally determined variables, the size of a space and the materials from which it is made, introduced a new confidence into auditorium design. Since then acoustics has become one of the most sophisticated branches of building science and the basic parameters of the acoustically good auditorium have been established.

Few twentieth-century auditoria suggest, at first sight, much dependency on the historical precedents defined above and one might suppose that this reflects the contribution of science. Closer examination reveals that science has primarily helped to explain why the precedents were successful, rather than to define a fundamentally new basis for design, free from the traditional empirical constraints on form. With the assistance of science the evolutionary process has certainly accelerated, but it is still possible to indicate the formal antecedents of most designs. At the Royal Festival Hall in London designed by a team led by Leslie Martin at the London County Council and completed in 1951 (Figure 4.9), the most vital question, that of the form of the auditorium, was referred back to the relative certainty of precedent.

## Analysis, synthesis and speculation

There are two interrelated reasons why explanatory theory has not ousted precedent in design: first, the nature of the scientific method itself and, second, the nature of the activity of design. The method of classical science, as Wittkower observed, is to reduce reality to its constituent parts and to make explicit certain fundamental relationships of cause and effect. For our purposes Sabine's equation of reverberation time $R = 0.16 \, V/A$ is an ideal example of this.

The problems of architectural design are of a different order. The parameters of Sabine's equation, the volume (V) and absorption (A) of a space, depend fundamentally upon properties of that space and can only be derived from a quite detailed description of it. Described only in Sabine's terms, spaces that in all other respects are totally dissimilar could be taken to be identical. In other words, the reductionist procedures of classical science lead us to a level of abstraction that is remote from many architectural concerns.

The other side of this coin directs attention towards the nature of design as an activity. Here, probably the most significant development in design theory in recent years has been the formal acknowledgement of the role of precedent by such writers as Colquhoun, Broadbent and March,[4] and the attempts, particularly by the latter in his PDI model of design, to show how this relates to the products of building science and to the questions of values and norms. These contributions indicate the centrality of reference to a

4.6
Charles Garnier, Paris Opera, 1861–75.

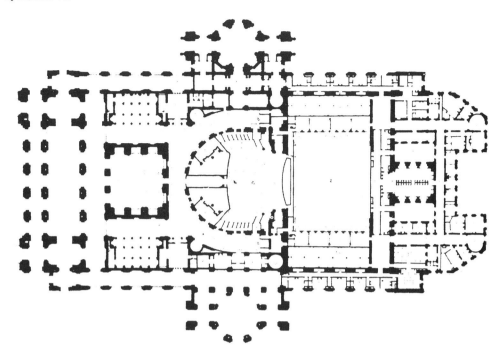

4.7
Otto Brückwald, Festspielhaus,
Bayreuth, 1876.

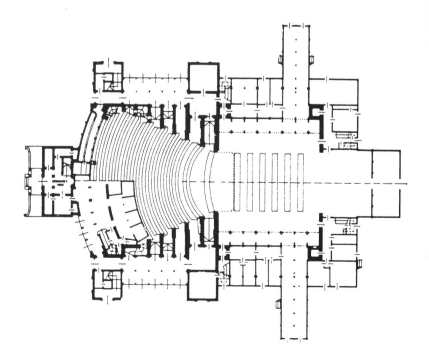

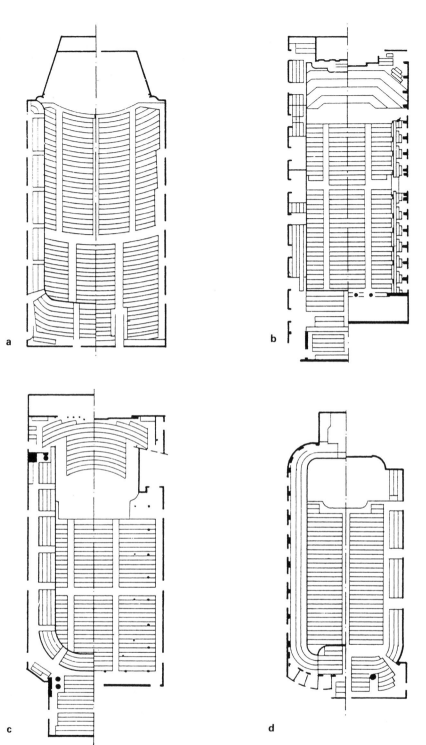

4.8
The 'shoebox' concert hall: a) Symphony
Hall, Boston; b) Grosser
Musikvereinssaal, Vienna; c) St
Andrew's Hall, Glasgow; d) Neues
Gewandhaus, Leipzig.

a

b

c

d

4.9
Leslie Martin and others, Royal Festival
Hall, London, 1951.

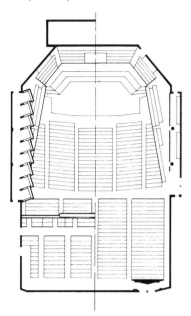

## Notes and references

1
Vitruvius, *Ten Books on Architecture*,
Morgan, M.H. (trans.), Dover, New
York, 1960.

2
Wittkower, R., *Architectural Principles
in the Age of Humanism*, London,
Tiranti, 1962.

3
Sabine, W.C., 'Reverberation', in *The
American Architect*, 1900. Reprinted in
Hunt, F. (ed.), *Collected Papers on
Acoustics*, Dover, New York, 1964.

4
Colquhoun, A., 'Typology and design
method', *Arena*, June, 1967; Broadbent,
G., *Design in Architecture*, John Wiley
and Sons, London, 1973; March, L.,
'The logic of design and the question of
value', in March, L. (ed.) *The
Architecture of Form*, Cambridge
University Press, Cambridge, 1976.

5
Willey, H.B., 'A theoretical framework
of environmental control of buildings',
PhD dissertation (unpublished),
University of Cambridge, 1978.

6
Banham, R., *The Architecture of the
Well-tempered Environment*,
Architectural Press, London, 1969.

comprehensive, if generalized, conception of a design in the production of a particular case. This reference comprehends the values and norms of the case and defines the parameters of the essential technical analysis which most modern buildings demand.

This model of the situation implies that the role of 'scientific' research in architecture, as opposed to building science, is first to establish a morphology of architectural form and then to use the tools of building science and other methods of analysis to make explanatory statements about the relationship between form and performance. As a practical programme this has the attraction of offering a more structured basis for the application of traditional analytical research. This has generally been conducted on an *ad hoc* basis. Little attempt has been made to use analytical models to make statements about the relative performance of ranges of designs in a way that will aid designers in the selection of appropriate precedents or types. But beyond this there is another contribution which this research can make. This is to investigate forms which the essentially conservative process of precedent-based design has not produced, but which are implicit in the morphology. This is a more speculative activity and requires research to break out from its predominantly analytical mode and to explore new relationships between form and performance which might be suggested by the insights offered by research.

As an indication of what might be possible, consider Willey's discussion of environmental design in office buildings.[5] This plots the principal office building 'stereotypes' on a 'solution space', defined in terms of the degree of control allowed to the occupants and the relationship between the building envelope and mechanical systems (filter/switch) (Figures 8.1, 8.2). The analysis, which also shows the archetypal cave and campfire used by Banham,[6] indicates a large region within which no strong stereotype has emerged. Inventive speculative research could examine the forms which lie in this area and thus influence practice through the proposal of novel designs whose performance could be compared with that of the 'standard' precedents.

The evidence of the history of auditorium design indicates the importance of precedent in design. It also, in the more recent past, shows how the 'scientific method' has only a limited influence on the further evolution of building typology. If we are to demonstrate the value of architectural research it is essential that it should be seen to influence design. To achieve this it is vital that research should become actively involved in making clear the formal possibilities that follow from a deeper understanding of the elements of architecture.

# 5 Objective knowledge and the art and science of architecture

> The ultimate object of design is form, physical clarity cannot be achieved in a form until there is first some programmatic clarity in the designer's mind and actions; and for this to be possible, in turn, the designer must first trace his design problem to its earliest functional origins and be able to find some sort of pattern in them.

With these words Christopher Alexander began his book *Notes on the Synthesis of Form*.[1] The book became one of the seminal documents of the design method school, which was one of the dominant themes of architectural theory in the 1960s.

Alexander read both mathematics and architecture at Cambridge University before moving to the USA where he undertook the work on the doctoral thesis that, eventually, became this book. It would be a mistake, however, to assume that his work has a close affinity with the line of research which has evolved since the late 1960s in the Cambridge School, under the initial influence of Leslie Martin. Indeed the work of what is now called the Martin Centre may be more accurately represented as a process of systematic criticism of the more mechanistic elements of modern movement dogma and, hence, of the theories of the design method school.

The aims of this essay are to summarize the main elements of this critique and, then, to show how it may be possible to establish a basis for the production of works of architecture which reconciles the conventionally incompatible qualities of intuition and rationality, of art and science.

The central preoccupation of the design method movement was, as the name implies, the study of the process of design. Its achievement was the proposition of a number of models of the process.[2] These, in spite of detailed differences between them, shared a general form in which design is said to proceed from *analysis* through *synthesis* to *evaluation* and, then, to repeat the process until a satisfactory solution is reached. Now, any experienced designer will recognize something about the way he or she works in these models, but will also recognize that the models fail to deal with the crucial question. This concerns not *how* but *what* to design.

In 1967 Alan Colquhoun published his important essay, 'Typology and design method'.[3] In this he discussed the problem of the design method school's devotion to analysis of the architectural programme as the generator of form.

Many people believe, not without reason, that the intuitive methods of design traditionally used by architects are incapable of dealing with the complexity of the problems to be solved and that, without sharper tools of analysis and classification, the designer tends to fall back on previous examples for the solution of new problems, on type solutions.

Colquhoun quotes an observation by Tomas Maldonado, one of the 'high priests' of design methodology, that type-solutions 'were like a cancer on the body of the solution'.

Colquhoun goes on to develop a powerful critique of the cultural poverty, of the design method standpoint and thence to argue the significance of typology. In what follows I want to describe the work carried out in Cambridge that approaches the question of the relationship between the 'how' and the 'what' of architectural design in a different, but, I believe, complementary way.

In an essay published in 1976, Lionel March, then Director of the Martin Centre, began with a quotation from a paper by Christopher Alexander and Barry Poyner.

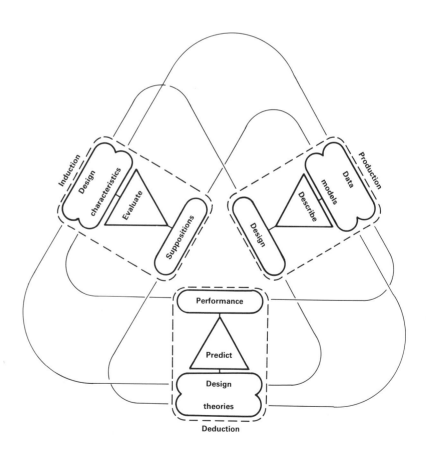

5.1
Model of rational design process.

We believe it is possible to define design in such a way that the rightness or wrongness of a building is clearly a question of fact, not a question of value.[4]

March points out the fallacy of this statement, even in the language of design method in which the term evaluation is, as we have seen, central to all models of design. More importantly, however, he goes on to propose a model of the design process in which he attempts to acknowledge the significance of the notion of type in architectural design and, thus, to resolve the problem identified by Colquhoun.

March's PDI model (Figure 5.1) is based on the philosophical work of Charles S. Peirce in which he identified distinct modes of reasoning: deductive, inductive and abductive. In Peirce's terms deduction proves something must be; induction shows that something actually is; abduction merely shows that something may be. By transformation and simplification March arrives at the basis of his model by proposing that production creates; deduction predicts; induction evaluates.

Hence the PDI model offers, however schematically, a representation of the design process in which creativity has a central place. This is quite unlike all previous models with their obsession with analysis and, thus, represents an important step forward. But in solving this problem March opens up a much more difficult issue. If the place of creativity is formally acknowledged we must offer some idea of its nature and its origins. We are, therefore, in very deep philosophical water!

Although it may not provide a complete answer to this question there is a substantial body of theoretical argument and empirical evidence to support the contention that production, in March's sense, relies substantially on the availability, and use, of type as a potent source of form in architecture. In 'Types, norms and habit' I attempted to show that the notion of the stereotype plays an important role in design. In my definition a stereotype 'is simply a generally held notion about the nature of a good solution to any . . . design problem that frequently inspires the initial design hypothesis . . . it plays a creative role by allowing the designer to begin the cycle of analysis and revision from a reasonably confident position'.

Now it may be possible to say that, even within the framework of a model such as March's, architecture is still regarded as primarily a mechanistic response to the 'facts' of the programme, and that the idea of type does not guarantee freedom from this. It is, perhaps, here where the question of value re-enters the discussion. In the context of the models of the design methodologists and the statements of Alexander, *et al.*, it is true that the cultural and historical sources of design have no formal recognition alongside programmatic statements of fact and their corollary of a primarily technological response. The true value of type, however, is that it is possible to interpret a single type of an extended typology from many points of view. It is just as valid to interpret a type representation of a building as a solution to a technical problem, say of acoustics, as a carrier of cultural or aesthetic meaning. This point may be demonstrated by considering the form of the opera house. Here the almost Darwinian ubiquity of the 'horseshoe' auditorium speaks of its acoustic utility, but equally we may reflect on the cultural associations of this form as a setting for the experience of theatre in all its multifarious dimensions.

It was precisely this wider potentiality of type that Colquhoun addressed in his essay in writing that,

artifacts have not only a 'use' value in the crudest sense but also an 'exchange' value . . . Whether the object was a cult image (say, a sculpture) or a kitchen utensil, it was an object of cultural exchange, and it formed part of a system of communication within society. Its 'message' value was precisely the image of the final form which the craftsman, held in his mind's eye as he was making it, and to which his artifact corresponded as closely as possible. In spite of the development of the scientific method, we must still attribute such social or iconic values to the products of technology and recognize that they play an essential role in the generation and development of the physical tools of our environment.

This 'image . . . held in [the] mind's eye' may take many forms in its function as a design stereotype, from extreme generalization to absolute precision. It may be the idea of the 'horseshoe' auditorium as a generator of a particular instance or it may, as in the case of Charles Garnier's Paris Opera, 1861–75, be a precise, pre-existing instance such as Victor Louis' Grand Theatre at Bordeaux, 1780, that was Garnier's direct dimensional model for his auditorium, and, thus, enabled him to overcome the frustrations of the 'bizarre science' of nineteenth-century acoustics. In the case of an architect confronted by a difficult problem such as the design of an acoustically satisfactory auditorium, in the period before modern building science it was clearly prudent to resort to replication of a demonstrably satisfactory precedent.

The instance of the acoustic design of auditoria serves to provide a vehicle by which to examine the way in which science, in a conventional Cartesian definition, relates to the production of form in architecture. The foundations of modern architectural acoustics were laid by W.C. Sabine at the turn of the century.[5] In his equation for the calculation of the reverberation time of a space Sabine established a precise relationship between that acoustic property and the relevant variables of the architecture, its dimensions, expressed as volume; and its materials, expressed as total acoustic absorption. There is, as we now know, much more to the design of an acoustically acceptable auditorium. Nonetheless, Sabine's work offered, at first sight, the opportunity to escape from what Maldonado would regard as the fetters of type and enter a new world of formal freedom. The experience of the intervening years has, however, shown the limitations of this kind of scientific understanding as a basis for architectural invention.

In Britain the Royal Festival Hall, 1951, was seen by its architects as an opportunity to translate the scientific allegiances of the modern movement from the realms of polemic into conscious and constructive application in design, art and science to be properly married. But, when it came to the most important question of all, what shape to make the auditorium, recourse was made to type, rather than risk the uncertainties of acoustic theory. The members of the design team most directly concerned with acoustic questions wrote,

The general shape of the Royal Festival Hall was for the most part a logical development from the acoustical requirements, with one exception, which was the choice of a plan . . . No decisive guidance on this point could be obtained from acoustical theory, and it was decided therefore to fall back upon tradition. The evidence seemed to point to halls with parallel sides having generally better reputations for musical acoustics . . .[6]

So, after half a century of the development of acoustical science, theory had to give way to type. The ability to specify the desired reverberation time at a number of frequencies, to relate this to the properties of the materials from which the auditorium would be constructed, and to a generalized description of its geometry, its volume, were an inadequate basis from which to work. Only when a form is selected may the process of analysis and evaluation begin, exactly as described by March's PDI model. This is not surprising if we consider the necessarily reductionist process of simplification implicit in all conventional scientific procedures. These inevitably lead to a degree of abstraction from which it is impossible to construct an artefact as complex as even the simplest building.

So, if we accept the centrality of the idea of type in architectural design, what does this suggest for the development of architectural studies? In 'Types, norms and habit', I suggested that the shortcomings of the conventional use of stereotype – there is a tendency for one type to predominate at any particular time – places undue limitation on the design process. I went on to suggest that, 'there is, in fact, a store of accumulated experience which contains all previous solutions (types) and which will be enlarged in the future'.

This proposition carries implications of a kind of architectural Darwinism and calls to mind the proposition advanced as long ago as 1912 by the British architect W.R. Lethaby that,

Modern builders need a classification of architectural factors irrespective of time and country, a classification by essential variation. Some day we shall get a morphology of the art by some architectural Linnaeus or Darwin, who will start from the simple cell and relate to it the most complex structures . . . So long as the whole field of past architectural experiment is presented to us accidentally only under historical schedules, designing architecture is likely to be conceived as scholarship rather than as the adaptation of its accumulated powers to immediate needs.[7]

Lethaby's proposition anticipated, albeit naively, Karl Popper's theory of objective knowledge.[8] In this Popper postulates the existence of three 'worlds': World 1, an objective world of material things; World 2, a subjective world of minds; World 3, a world of objective structures which are the products, not necessarily intentional, of minds or living creatures, but which, once produced, exist independently of them.

Popper suggests that forerunners of these objective structures may be found in the animal kingdom in the nests of birds, spiders' webs, and so forth, which are built by the animal outside its body in order to solve its problems. In the world of humankind Popper sees World 3 structures in more abstract terms in such phenomena as language, ethics, law, religion, philosophy, the sciences, the arts and institutions, our whole cultural heritage. These are, for him, encoded in World 1 objects such as brains, books, pictures, films, indeed records of all kinds. In my mind this clear distinction between the abstraction of World 3 structures and the materiality of World 1 contradicts the idea of animal's nests, webs and so forth as existing in World 3 and leaves the question of the location of buildings in Popper's worlds unresolved. However, Popper's suggestion that World 3 constructs, whether in their pure abstract form, or as encoded in World 1 artefacts, have a value beyond that of the minds of their creators is particularly appealing when applied to the use of type in the process of architectural design.

Philip Steadman has written extensively on the subject of evolution in design.[9] Taking his cue from Lethaby and Popper he has written that,

morphology as a study of abstract possibilities of spatial arrangement . . . can only proceed so far before the question arises "How can the range of possible forms be restricted?"

He suggests that the answer can only be found by reference to 'architectural' properties, and that these may only be defined by making reference to architectural history.

This raises the exciting possibility of a collaboration between the worlds of architectural history, design theory and, ultimately of crucial importance, of practice. In this, the aims and methods of each could come together, united in the common purpose of making the use of historical data relevant to the solution of problems of contemporary design, with equal relevance to both the technical realm of what is normally termed 'building science' and the complex cultural issues to which Colquhoun, among others, draws our attention. In this way the crippling barrier between art and science in architectural debate may be broken down.

## Notes and references

1
Alexander, C., *Notes in the Synthesis of Form*, Harvard University Press, Cambridge, Mass, 1967.

2
For a summary of these see Broadbent, G., *Design in Architecture*, John Wiley and Sons, London and New York, 1973.

3
Colquhoun, A., 'Typology and design method', *Arena*, June 1967.

4
March, L., 'The logic of design and the question of value', in March, L. (ed.), *The Architecture of Form*, Cambridge University Press, Cambridge, 1976.

5
Sabine, W.C., 'Reverberation', *American Architect*, vol. xx, 1900. Reprinted in Hunt, F. (ed.), *Collected Papers on Acoustics*, Dover, New York, 1964.

6
Allen, W.A. and Parkin, P.H., 'The Royal Festival Hall: acoustics and sound exclusion', *Architectural Review*, June 1951.

7
Lethaby, W.R., Architecture: *an Introduction to the History and Theory of the Art of Building*, Williams and Northgate, London, 1912.

8
Popper, K., *Objective Knowledge: an Evolutionary Approach*, Oxford University Press, Oxford, 1972.

9
Steadman, P., *The Evolution of Designs*, Cambridge Architectural and Urban Studies, Cambridge University Press, Cambridge, 1979.

71 | The art and science of architecture

# Space for services: the architectural dimension

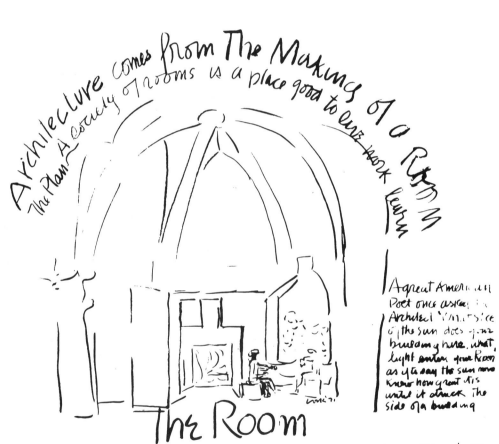

## The architectural dimension

I do not like ducts, I do not like pipes. I hate them really thoroughly, but because I hate them so thoroughly, I feel that they have to be given their place. If I just hated them and took no care, I think that they would invade the building and completely destroy it. I want to correct any notion you may have that I am in love with that kind of thing.[1]

In this statement Louis Kahn summarized the problem that confronts any architect who is called upon to design a highly serviced building. Modern servicing systems can account for a third or more of the total capital cost of a building. They can also make considerable demands for space within the building, in the total volume required and the accommodation of their distribution throughout the building. Viewed historically these services are a relatively recent development in building technology and, by their essentially mechanical nature, they differ fundamentally from all the other elements and components from which a building is assembled. So we may readily agree with Kahn 'that they have to be given their place'.

The unanswered question, of course, is how may we give services their place? What are the essential architectural characteristics of a highly serviced building? To what extent does the efficient design of service systems influence the form, even the appearance, of a building?

## The origins of services

Building services, in the modern sense of the term, developed in the wake of the Industrial Revolution. It is clear from a large number of sources[2] that the idea of the use of a circulating system of piped steam had its origins in the eighteenth century and that the use of gas lighting in buildings quickly followed the first street lighting installation in Pall Mall in 1807. These had the effect of liberating the use of buildings from the constraints of the naturally occurring environment. It was now possible to ignore the cold and the darkness and to make fuller use of buildings than ever before. The benefits of this step ensured that all future buildings would be required to accommodate environmental service systems, and these were soon joined by other devices for the transport of people and materials.[3]

What is often not appreciated is how early all of the apparatus of building services was accepted into everyday practice. Although the full impact of the introduction of electricity did not occur until the last decade of the century, following Swan and Edison's invention of the incandescent lamp in 1879, the idea of comprehensive servicing was well established by the middle of the century.

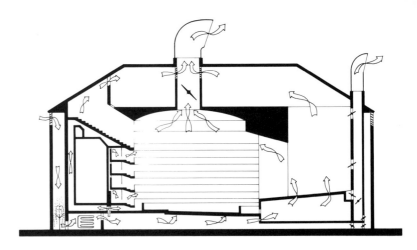

This profound change in the use and the technology of buildings was assimilated into the intellectual and physical fabric of architecture with virtually no visual or stylistic effect. This was not, as may be thought, because architects disregarded the demands of the new technologies, leaving them to their engineering advisers. On the contrary, there is much evidence to show that many of the major architects of this period frequently took the initiative in technical matters. It was the product of their attitude to the relationship between building technology and the appearance of buildings. Technology was seen as a means, not as an end. Architects were thus able to find unobtrusive ways of incorporating complex and often bulky systems into the fabric (Figure 6.1).

In the twentieth century this homogeneity of conception and realization has been broken up progressively. This process has frequently been justified by an implied history in which large-scale building services are claimed to be a recent invention. But Reyner Banham, as long ago as 1969, wrote,

Historically . . . the architecture of making manifest environmental services had to wait upon a change of *aesthetic* [my italics] preferences quite as much as upon the growing difficulties of finding somewhere to hide the ducting and mechanical plant . . .[4]

With the evidence of nineteenth-century building practice before us, it is timely to take a new and broader view of the whole question of the role and nature of services raised by Kahn's *cri de cœur*.

### Aesthetic preference

To a nineteenth-century architect, the role of service systems was to supplement the historic environmental functions of the building fabric. The idea that services might completely replace some of these functions is unique to the twentieth-century. Therefore, highly serviced buildings in the nineteenth century were conceived in fundamentally different terms from many late twentieth-century examples. This difference may be expressed in two ways. First, in the environmental vision it embodied, and second, in the attitude to the physical incorporation of the services in the fabric of the building.

Sir Charles Barry's involvement with the problems of introducing service systems into early Victorian buildings is now well documented. In the Houses of Parliament of 1835–52 (Figure 6.2) and the Reform Club of 1841 (Figure 6.3) we can see how Barry approached the environmental and the technological aspects of his service systems.[5] The environmental key to the planning of both buildings is the need to achieve good natural lighting in all the major rooms and in the circulation routes. The whole environmental scheme follows from this. These buildings are thus tied to the preoccupation with natural lighting which is such an important part of all the treatises on architecture, from Vitruvius, through Alberti and Palladio to the British versions by writers such as William Chambers and Robert Morris.

In both of these buildings, the problems of heating and especially ventilation were regarded as of great importance. The Houses of Parliament had had a long and difficult history of attempting satisfactorily to ventilate the debating chambers, and the Reform Club building committee expressed its interest in the subject early

6.2
Sir Charles Barry, Houses of Parliament, London, 1835–52. River front heating and ventilating system. Cross-section.

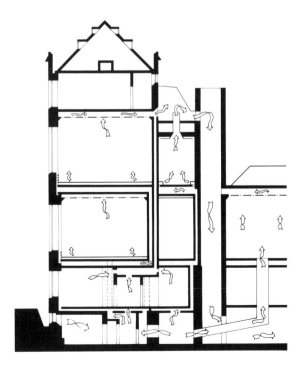

in its discussions with Barry. The uppermost environmental concern in each case was to bring fresh air into the building without causing draughts.

This was achieved by distributing fresh, warmed air through a network of ducts and flues incorporated into the walls, floors and roof structures. An important consideration on the extract side of the systems was the removal of the products of combustion from gas lighting. Although the buildings were mainly daylit, their use after nightfall demanded the best available artificial lighting.

### Environmental quality

The environmental approach in these buildings by Barry was to extend the potential of the unaided building fabric by unobtrusively incorporating new technologies. The quality of the environment combined the virtues of traditional daylit interiors with the extension of use offered by artificial lighting and, on the thermal side, provided a comfortable temperature throughout the year and a consistent supply of fresh air. A similar concern for the avoidance of the display of mere technical innovation was demonstrated in the manner in which the systems were housed.

At the Reform Club, Barry made effective use of hollow *poches*, or solid corners, to conceal his ducts. The fact that the air was propelled through the system by a steam-driven fan relieved him of having to raise natural draught stacks to a great height in order to

6.3
Sir Charles Barry, Reform Club, London, 1841. Plan.

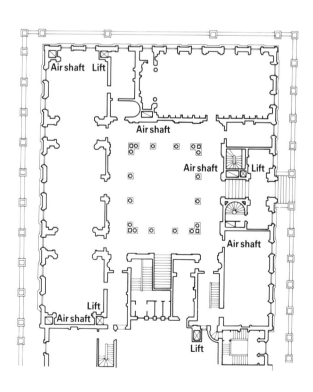

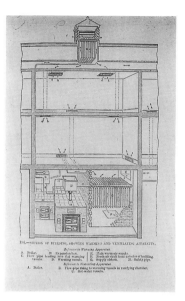

achieve sufficient extract velocity, which could well have led to serious compositional difficulties for the adoption of the Renaissance palazzo as his model. On the other hand, this problem was brilliantly reconciled with his, and Pugin's, Gothic ambitions at the Houses of Parliament.

Environmental principles and systems of this kind became commonplace in the nineteenth century in buildings as diverse as Alfred Waterhouse's Natural History Museum in London of 1873–81 and his Manchester Assize Courts of 1859, many theatres, including Semper's opera houses at Dresden of 1841 and Vienna of 1871[6] and the numerous school buildings[7] constructed in the years following the Education Act of 1870 (Figure 6.4).

At the Glasgow School of Art of 1907, Charles Rennie Mackintosh adopted an environmental philosophy that differed little from Barry's installations in a building of very different aesthetic ambitions (Figure 6.5). The predominance of natural lighting is apparent from the variety of window types and sizes and the widespread use of roof-lighting. This is particularly evident from the cross-sections in which daylighting considerations explain the location of spaces and the many setbacks and projections. This building was electrically lit and Mackintosh seized the opportunity to explore the decorative as well as the functional possibilities of this quite new technology. Heating was by fan-driven, warm air with a duct network similar to those in the buildings discussed above. There was, however, a clearer expression of the grilles and ductwork in the more utilitarian areas of the building, such as the studios, although Mackintosh remained as discreet as his Victorian forebears about these matters in the more public and finished rooms.

### Servicing modernism

As the twentieth century progressed, the technology of environmental services was gradually refined, particularly with respect to artificial lighting, power distribution and control systems. The fluorescent lamp, which produces high levels of light for very low power consumption, has allowed buildings to free themselves from the need to ensure that all important spaces are daylit. The potential of these developments for new forms of expression was gradually realized and exploited by many architects, as Banham has comprehensively documented. But the first phase of this development was subsumed in the pursuit of the idea of an architecture of glass in which the clarity of the idea, as first represented in Mies van der Rohe's glass skyscraper projects, overrode all other concerns. In this minimalist environmental vision the services had to be as discreet as those in Victorian buildings.

Beneath the radical transformation of the aesthetic, the physical

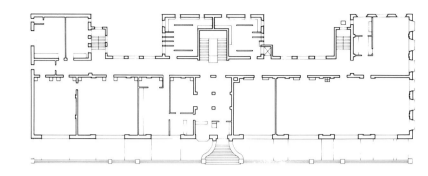

6.5
C.R. Mackintosh, Glasgow School of
Art, 1907. Plan.

6.6
Louis Kahn, Richards Memorial
Laboratories, Philadelphia, 1961.

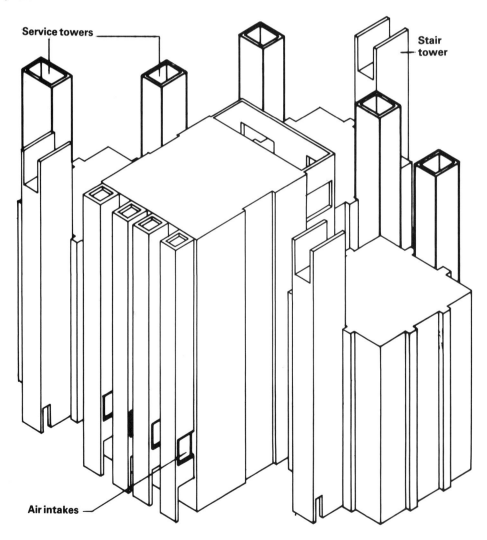

concealment of services was still regarded as a priority. This was normally achieved by the adoption of the continuous suspended ceiling to define an unobstructed service void at each level. There was, however, one fundamental difference between these buildings and their predecessors. Their very occupation *depended* upon the use of services. A simple glass wall is inherently a poor environmental barrier at any time of the year, and the all-glass building requires a continuous input of an artificially created environment. Attempts to minimize the thermal problems of the glass wall, by the use of tinted or coated glass, led glass architecture to the paradox of the permanent use of artificial lighting. The intimate connection between the external climate and the environment within buildings, which had existed throughout the history of architecture, was thus severed.

In the period following the Second World War the other theme of twentieth-century environmental design gathered pace. This was the urge to give service systems direct expression. The seminal building in this development was Louis Kahn's 1961 Richards Memorial Laboratories in Philadelphia. By placing all the vertical services, including staircases and lifts, in shafts grouped around the perimeter of the square-plan laboratories, Kahn achieved a clarity of expression and eloquence of composition which had wide appeal (Figure 6.6). When this was consolidated by his slogan differentiating between 'served' and 'servant' spaces, the die was cast for the abandonment of the historically subservient role of service systems in architecture.

Many of the developments of the high-tech school of the 1970s would not have taken place in the way they did had Kahn not so clearly articulated these principles at Richards, nor had Banham so persuasively explained their roots and potential in *The Architecture of the Well-tempered Environment*. The line of descent from Richards to Piano and Rogers' Pompidou Centre in Paris of 1977 and Rogers' Lloyd's Building in London of 1984 is absolutely clear.

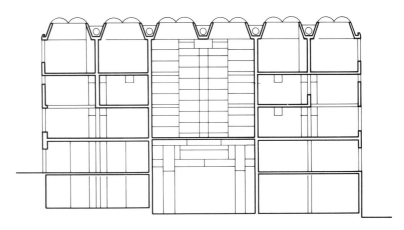

6.7
Louis Kahn, Mellon Center, Yale University, New Haven, 1974. Cross-section.

What is not so clear, however, is that Kahn did not regard the Richards building as a model for all building types, only as a necessity when confronted by the extremely complex servicing demands of a scientific research laboratory. In other words, Kahn's attitude to services, both to their function and expression, was very complex and refined, as can be shown by analysing his buildings for other uses.

In this context a comparison between Kahn's Mellon Center at Yale University and Piano and Rogers' Pompidou Centre is irresistible. The buildings were designed within two years of each other, Mellon in 1969, Pompidou in 1971. Both are simple rectangles in plan, have expressed structural frames, and are fully air-conditioned. Mellon is much the smaller building and had a simpler brief in the sense that it was not called upon to house such a diversity of uses as at Pompidou. But they are both primarily buildings for the accommodation and display of works of art. Why then are they so strikingly different in their approaches to the nature of the internal environment and to the role of servicing systems both inside and out (Figures 6.7 and 6.8)?

Kahn's approach is concisely stated in his sketch of 'The Room' made in 1971 (Figure 6.9). At the foot of this he wrote, 'A room is not a room without natural light. Natural light gives the time of day and the mood of the seasons to enter'.[8] Speaking of the Pompidou Centre, Renzo Piano has said,

There is the relish for the polemical, the provocative, the sending up of the accepted idea of a museum and what it is meant to be. At the start of the '70s we were at a crossroad, we had to choose between two different concepts of culture; either institutional, esoteric, intimidating, or something unofficial, open and accessible to the general public. We opted for the latter . . . The building is a diagram. People read it in a flash. Its 'viscera' are on the outside, you see it all, understand the way people get around it, its lifts and escalators.[9]

In his statement Kahn was reaching back to the tradition of the daylit building, even though the Mellon Center is demonstrably of its own time. Piano and Rogers, on the other hand, set out deliberately to provoke, and chose to use the technology of the building, its 'viscera', as the instrument of their iconoclasm. In Kahn's building the primacy of natural light in the environmental scheme established a qualitative concern with the internal environment. In designing an art museum he established an order for the services which, while it is clear, systematic and accessible, was totally subservient to his concern with quality. For Piano and Rogers the concern was more with the display of the technology of environmental control than with the resultant environment. What has been reluctantly accepted by Kahn at the Richards Memorial

81 | Space for services: the architectural dimension

Laboratories in order to prevent the services 'destroying' the building, at Pompidou became an end in itself.

Throughout the Mellon Center the major rooms are lit by windows or rooflights, or by a combination of the two. Technically this provides a range of lighting conditions for the pictures. Subjectively, the experience is closer to a walk through an English country house than a machine for viewing pictures. On the other hand, the concerns of conservation and environmental control are satisfied by the air-conditioning system. This is accommodated in centrally placed vertical ducts, hollow floor slabs and in the coffers of the roof structure, upon which are placed the rooflights with their external solar shades. The system is simple, efficient and unobtrusive.

At the Pompidou Centre the principal gallery spaces are artificially lit and the unashamed expression of structure and services on the exterior is continued inside. The inspiration for the approach was the idea of flexibility: 'nothing is rigid, immutable, the container is flexible, adaptable through the use of "soft" mechanisms, articulated so that it can be adapted to rapid developments in information systems and communications.'[10] In these circumstances the interior of the building inevitably becomes general rather than specific and this means that the services must be organized in a way which allows them to be adapted to unpredictable change.

The validity of the approach might be said to be demonstrated by the way in which the fourth floor of the building was transformed by Gae Aulenti in 1985 (Figure 6.10). The original free-plan arrangement has been replaced by a highly structured sequence of rooms, which takes the major structural bay of the building as its principal determinant. The lighting is incorporated in the walls of the new enclosures, rather than on grids in the ceiling structure as before, and by reflecting off ceiling panels, simulates the lighting quality found in many traditional daylit galleries. Because the partitions stop short of the floor structure above, the air-conditioning plant continues to operate without modification. The transformation is radical and ingenious. But it is ironic that its major achievement is to approximate an approach to museum design that was so emphatically rejected by the original architects.

It is clear from this comparison that the expression of service systems in the manner of the Pompidou Centre is not the necessary result of either the programme of the modern museum building or the demands of the apparatus of environmental control plant itself. In technical terms, the Mellon Center provides an equally suitable physical environment for the display of works of art, with plant which operates in a similar way using similar components. What is different, therefore, is the aesthetic posture assumed by the architects and its implications for the way in which they view the internal environment (Figure 6.11).

For Kahn, the challenge was to use the technologies of his own time to produce a building that retained the qualities of an earlier building tradition. As we have seen, the need to achieve good natural lighting has been fundamental in building throughout history. It continued to be a paramount consideration through all nineteenth-century developments in building technology. This link was only severed after the Second World War when the combination of air conditioning and the fluorescent lamp made possible the deep-plan, totally artificial environment building. In this, as at the Pompidou Centre, the environment becomes a question of engineering calculation rather than of architectural judgement. The connection between this point of view and the desire to make the building into a piece of engineering display is easy to see. Piano has stated that: 'if anything is worth copying it is the design procedure, the scientific approach, the technical research'.

This difference in approach may be discovered in all kinds of buildings. For example, a comparison between Arup Associates' Gateway Two office building in Basingstoke of 1983 and Richard Rogers' Lloyd's Building reveals an equally clear distinction in a building type that may, at first sight, appear to offer less scope for alternative interpretation than an art museum. Isn't the office function, after all, inherently prosaic and technologically dominated (Figures 6.12 and 6.13)?

At Lloyd's, the significance of the servicing function is as vigorously expressed as at the Pompidou Centre. The building incorporates many innovations in the mechanisms of environmental control, which will certainly become part of the commonplace air-conditioning equipment of the future, particularly for local environmental control.

At Gateway Two, on the other hand, there is no obvious display and environmental control is achieved with surprisingly modest technical resources. Instead of using a network of enclosed ducts to supply and extract conditioned air, the whole building has, in effect, become a duct through which natural ventilation takes place, providing sufficient fresh air in winter and summer, and preventing overheating in the summer. Winter warmth is provided by a simple hot-water central heating system. The building has virtually no specifically designated service zones, except for raised floors to contain power supplies and data links for the office equipment.

Again, the striking differences between the approach to servicing in these buildings arises more from the predispositions of their designers than from any compelling issues in either brief. The technical effectiveness of either design is not questioned.

6.10
Gae Aulenti, Pompidou Centre, Paris,
1985. Detail of gallery installation.

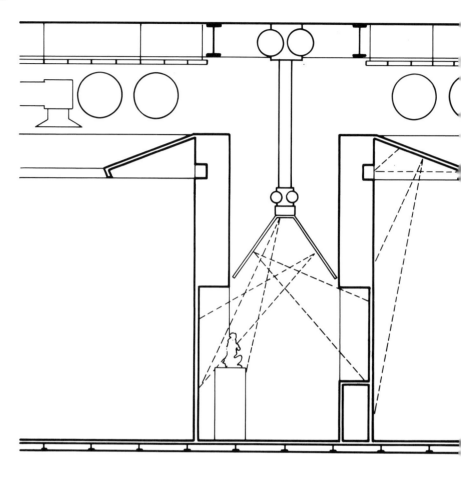

6.11
Louis Kahn, Mellon Center, Yale
University, New Haven, 1974. Roof
detail.

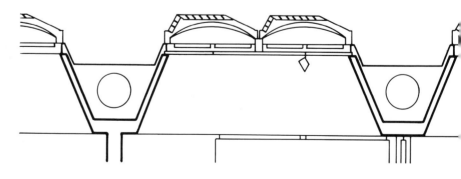

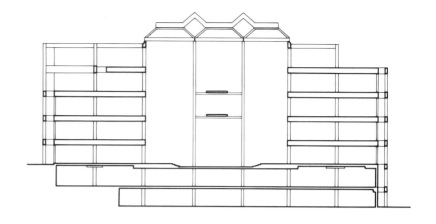

6.12
Arup Associates, Gateway Two,
Basingstoke, 1983. Cross-section.

6.13
Richard Rogers, Lloyd's Building,
London, 1984.

85 | Space for services: the architectural dimension

## Exclusive or selective

What these buildings and all the historical examples show is that there is no simple, single answer to the question, 'How do we give services their place?' We can, however, identify a number of considerations which bear upon the answer. The first is the nature of the environment which the building and its services provide. If this is predominantly artificial, that is, fully air-conditioned, artificially lit and automatically controlled, the implications for the services are quite different from those required if the building is naturally lit and ventilated. This is the difference between the exclusive and selective modes of environmental control.

Until the middle of the twentieth century all buildings, even those that had extensive service systems, were selective in their approach to environmental control. They admitted some element of the naturally occurring climate as an essential component of the internal environment.

The realization that an entire environment could be created by artificial means only came many years after it first became technically possible. What this exclusive mode did was break down the crucial relationship between environmental control and the form of a building. For this reason it is important, in beginning the design of a building, to be clear about the environmental philosophy to be adopted and the reasons for choosing it.

As a general rule, a selective building needs fewer services than an exclusive design, although it is hardly conceivable that any practical modern building would have no service systems.

Many selective buildings have extensive environmental services. In addition, we should not overlook the other kinds of services that are often required in many specialized buildings, such as laboratories and industrial buildings. An examination of the history of service design shows that complex and extensive systems have often been accommodated in buildings of many types, forms and styles for at least a century and a half.

The historical evidence shows that the effective design, installation, operation or maintenance of services may be achieved in many ways. The 'place' of services, in the sense that Kahn used the term, is therefore a matter of aesthetics rather than of overriding technical logic.

# Notes and references

1
Louis Kahn, quoted in *World Architecture 1*, Studio Books, London, 1964.

2
A useful summary of the origins of central heating is given in Harris, E., *Keeping Warm*, Victoria and Albert Museum, HMSO, London, 1982. By the early nineteenth century a large number of comprehensive treatises on the heating, ventilating and lighting of buildings had been published. For example, Reid, D.B., *Illustrations of the Theory and Practice of Ventilation*, Longman and Co., London, 1844; Tregold, T., *On the Principles and Practice of Warming and Ventilating Buildings*, Josiah Taylor, London, 1824; Laing, A., *Lighting*, Victoria and Albert Museum, HMSO, London, 1982.

3
Condit, C.W., *The Chicago School of Architecture*, University of Chicago Press, Chicago, 1964.

4
Banham, R. *The Architecture of the Well-Tempered Environment*, Architectural Press, London, 1969.

5
Olley, J., 'The Reform Club', *Architects' Journal*, 27 March 1985. Reprinted in Cruickshank, D. (ed.), *Timeless Architecture: 1*, Architectural Press, London, 1985.

6
A detailed description of Semper's achievements as an environmental designer may be found in Sachs, E.O., *Modern Opera Houses and Theatres* (3 vols), London, 1896–98.

7
These are fully described in *School Architecture*, Robson, E.R., London, 1874. Reprinted with an introduction by Malcolm Seaborne, Leicester University Press, Leicester 1972.

8
Giurgola, R. and Mehta, J. *Louis I. Kahn, Architect*, Westview Press, Boulder, Colorado, 1975.

9
Dini, M., *Renzo Piano, Projects and Buildings 1964–1983*, Electa/ Architectural Press, London, 1984.

10
*Architectural Review*, November 1985.

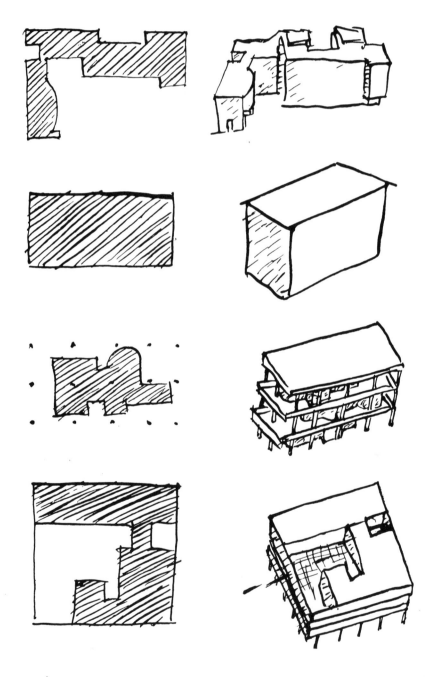

Throughout history a fundamental purpose of architecture has been to provide shelter. In modern buildings this is achieved by a combination of the historic protective function and the application of mechanical systems of environmental control. It is these systems that are the principal users of energy in buildings.

The application of scientifically based methods of analysis to building design first emerged in the nineteenth century, hand-in-hand with developments in building technology. But these had little visible impact on an architecture preoccupied with style. In the twentieth century the theoretical basis of the modern movement, however, explicitly embraced the ideas and implications of the scientific method.

The growth of concern with the question of energy conservation in buildings has coincided with widespread re-evaluation of the tenets of the modern movement. An element of this critique has been to question the validity of the scientific model in architecture. This essay argues that a synthesis of art and science is both possible and necessary in the production of architecture.

## Machine age theory

The relation of construction to design is the fundamental problem of architectural aesthetics.

The above quote is from Geoffrey Scott, writing in 1914.[1] His question of how to relate construction, technology and science to design is a recurrent theme in the theory of architecture. Scott's purpose in drawing attention to the matter was to rebut what he defined as the 'mechanical fallacy'. This was the proposition, with its roots in the writings of Pugin and Ruskin, that the structure and construction of a building should be clearly expressed.

In doing this Scott was playing one of the last and, in many respects, the winning cards in the style debate that had raged in England throughout the nineteenth century.[2] His preference for a revived classicism as the basis for the design of twentieth-century buildings depended on the disconnection of the appearance of a building from its method of construction. However, at the same time, a radically different view was emerging elsewhere in Europe.

Fernand Léger, writing in 1913, perceived the emergence of a new set of relationships between architecture and society and, implicitly, between aesthetic aims and technical means:

Architecture . . . is emerging from several centuries of false traditionalism and approaching a modern and utilitarian idea of its function . . . The modern conception of art . . . is the total expression of a new generation *whose condition it shares and whose aspirations it answers* [my italics].[3]

The adventure of the modern movement was rich and complex; it touched upon, and was touched by almost every facet of culture, but architecture made a special contribution by applying new technologies and elements of scientific thinking to the development of a new aesthetic. The essence of this is encapsulated in the writings of architects and architectural theorists in the 1920s and 1930s. Le Corbusier, for example, expressed it thus:

There is a new spirit: it is a spirit of construction and of synthesis guided by a clear conception. Whatever may be thought of it, it animates today the greater part of human activity.[4]

## New approaches

This new conception of the relationship between ends and means was quickly felt in the designs of pioneering architects. In '5 points d'une architecture nouvelle',[5] Le Corbusier showed how new approaches to construction could be applied to the problems of support, enclosure, planning and daylighting to produce a radically new result (Figure 7.1).

In addition to these demonstrations of the possibilities of new approaches to structure and construction, the modern movement also made explorations into the application of new technology to the problem of controlling the physical environment in buildings. Again Le Corbusier was at the forefront of these developments and applied the idea of the 'neutralizing wall', devised in collaboration with the physicist Gustave Lyon, to a number of projects, most notably to the Cité de Réfuge in Paris of 1932 (Figure 7.2).

In these developments new technologies were used as vital instruments in the production of a new aesthetic which was capable of expressing the aspirations of the new century. As Pevsner declared in *Pioneers of Modern Design*:

The Modern Movement in architecture, in order to be fully expressive of the twentieth century, had to possess both qualities, the faith in science and technology, in social science and rational planning, and the romantic faith in speed and the roar of machines.[6]

But this relationship may also be represented in another way. J.M. Richards claimed, in 1940:

The tendency . . . is for scientific progress to outstrip the ability to apply it. That is what happened in the last century: inventions kept piling up, to the confusion of architect, builder and public, who had no clear enough architectural philosophy to enable them to use them intelligently. Modern architecture is setting about the task of making something good and coherent out of what science offers.[7]

In the field of energy-conscious building design, it is clear that the pioneering buildings were conceived within the paradigm of the modern movement. Designs such as the Trombe–Michel house at Odeillo in France of 1967 (Figure 7.3), and the 1961 Wallasey School, Wirral, by Emslie A. Morgan (Figure 7.4), are clearly modernist, with their explicit relationship between form and technical function.

Just when these buildings were being completed, however, a new strand began to appear in practice and in critical discussion. In an essay first published in 1962, Alan Colquhoun observed that:

One of the remarkable facts about the architecture of the mid-twentieth century is that so many of its buildings exploit heavy and traditional methods of construction. From the point of view of building technique this would seem to be a regression from the ideals of the early period of the Modern Movement.[8]

The argument goes on to propose that the true value of new technology to the modern movement lay in the *idea* of it, rather than in the *fact*. The theory also proposes that the appeal of the buildings produced was 'due more to their success as symbolic representations than to the extent to which they solved technical problems'.

Colquhoun had detected in 1962 that the necessary conditions for the modern movement, in its original sense, no longer existed:

It is as if the urge to create the world anew by means of structures which had the lightness and tenuousness of pure thought had given way to the desire to create solid hideouts of the human spirit in a world of uncertainty and change, each one in itself a microcosm of an ideal world.

**A modern framework**

Developments in the theory and practice of architecture since the 1960s have, in spite of a pervasive pluralism, served to reinforce the view that the relationship between technology and aesthetics cannot be viewed with the clarity that characterized the modern movement, however symbolic that clarity may have been. In particular there is a need to re-establish a link with the past after modernism's 'demand for an open breach with the past, or even the abolition of the past'.[9] It may seem that the conspicuous display of structural and mechanical services in a building such as Richard Rogers' Lloyd's Building in London (Figure 7.5) demonstrates that the ideals of the modern movement have attained a new sophistication and expression in the work of the so-called 'high-tech' school. But the coexistence of this building alongside a design such as James Stirling and Michael Wilford's Staatsgallerie in Stuttgart of 1984 (Figure 7.6) demonstrates that such technical display does not have universal support.

7.1
Le Corbusier, four house types.

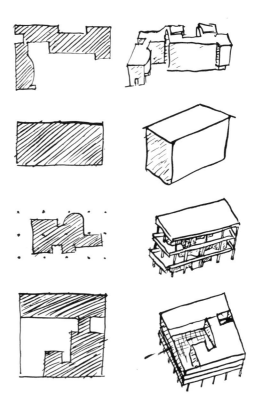

7.2
Le Corbusier, Cité de Réfuge, 1932.

7.3
Trombe–Michel house, Odeillo, 1967.

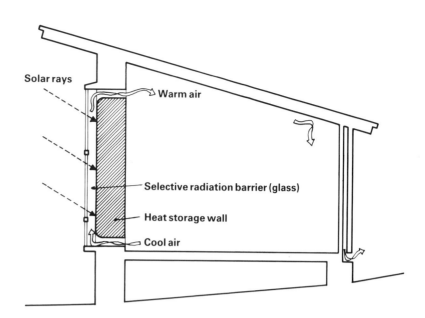

Solar rays

Warm air

Selective radiation barrier (glass)

Heat storage wall

Cool air

7.4
Emelie A. Morgan, St George's School,
Wallasey, 1961.

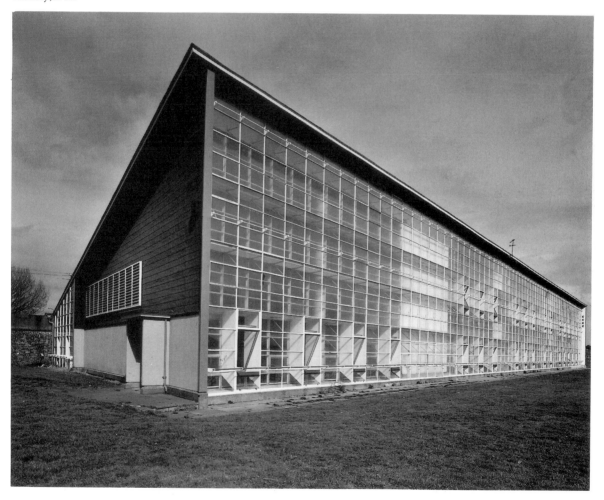

93 | The language barrier

7.5
Richard Rogers, Lloyd's Building,
London, 1984.

In addition, an apparent contradiction exists between the availability of a greater range of technologies than ever before, of a deeper scientific understanding of the physical processes that occur in buildings, of structural forces, environmental phenomena, and so forth, and the desire of many architects and society at large for architecture that no longer wears its technology on its sleeve. It is, arguably, more necessary than ever to make the best use of dwindling resources and, hence, not to abandon the tangible benefits of the application of science and technology in the production of architecture.

The modern movement created a framework, both literal and symbolic, within which this could be achieved. But it also created a language that now seems unable to cope with the very different expressive demands architecture is expected to address.

We need to reconsider the statement from Richards' *Introduction to Modern Architecture*, quoted above. He implied that, until the modern movement emerged, it was not possible even for the inventions of the nineteenth century to be applied in architecture. It is generally true that the full implications of new knowledge are only progressively appreciated, but it is a serious misrepresentation of the architecture of the nineteenth century to suggest that it failed to exploit the inventiveness of the scientists and technologists whose achievements wrought the Industrial Revolution.

There is overwhelming evidence, particulary from the researches of recent scholarship, that new constructional techniques and methods of heating and ventilating were quickly adopted by architects throughout Europe. These developments were not merely applied to provide useful marginal improvements of established forms, but also contributed to the development of an architectural language as different from that of the eighteenth century as the modern movement was from the nineteenth.

As early as 1843 Henri Labrouste, in his design for the Bibliothèque Ste Geneviève in Paris, 1843–50, used a cast-iron structure to new expressive ends. Later, at the Bibliothèque Nationale, also in Paris, 1858–68, Labrouste went further in exploring the functional and poetic potential of iron construction and the possibilities of a warm-air system of heating. The book stack for 900 000 volumes shows how new material and a well-defined functional requirement may come together with an eloquence that may be seen to anticipate the achievements of the modern movement. The main reading room, with its slender iron columns separating nine delicate roof-lit vaults, goes further still (Figure 7.7).

In London, architects such as Sir Charles Barry, in his work at the Reform Club of 1841 (Figure 7.8) and in the reconstruction of the Houses of Parliament of 1835–52, and Alfred Waterhouse at the Natural History Museum of 1873–81, (Figure 7.9)[10] also showed

7.6
James Stirling and Michael Wilford,
Staatsgalerie, Stuttgart, 1984.

94 | The Environmental Tradition

7.7
Henri Labrouste, Bibliothèque
Nationale, Paris, 1858–68.

7.8
Sir Charles Barry, Reform Club,
London, 1841. Detail.

7.9
Alfred Waterhouse, Natural History
Museum, London, 1873–81.

how the combination of stylistic historicism and new technology could result in cogent and original buildings.

Across Europe, in the work of architects as apparently diverse as Gottfried Semper, Victor Horta, Charles Rennie Mackintosh and many others, there is abundant proof that new technology and architectural design can be combined in a manner that does not require the overt technical determinism, which some adherents of the modern movement seem to have demanded.

This is not an argument for the adoption of nineteenth-century idioms to resolve the problems of the late twentieth century; revivalism is a blind alley. The point is to show that advanced, and often complex and bulky technology may be embodied in an architectural language that does not, on the surface at least, appear to be primarily concerned with such matters.

I have tried to show that the place of technology is not fixed in the syntax of architecture. The expressive needs of the modern movement (Gropius' 'new aspect of architecture corresponding to the technical civilization of the age we live in'[11]) required the unambiguous expression of technical means. If a more decorous architecture is now expected, it is surely possible to reconcile scientific thought and advanced technology without compromising their effectiveness, thus freeing the language to speak more effectively of other things.

# Notes and references

1
Scott, G., *The Architecture of Humanism*, Constable and Co., London, 1914.

2
See Macleod, R., *Style and Society: Architectural Ideology in Britain 1835–1914*, RIBA Publications, London. 1971.

3
Léger, F., 'The origins of painting and its representational value', *Montjoie!*, Paris, 1913. Reprinted in Fry, E.F., *Cubism*, Thames and Hudson, London, 1966.

4
Le Corbusier, Programme of *L'Espirit Nouveau*, No 1, October 1920.

5
Le Corbusier and Jeanneret, P., '5 points d'une architecture nouvelle', *Die Form*, vol. 2, 1972.

6
Pevsner, N., *Pioneers of Modern Design*, revised edition, Penguin Books, Harmondsworth, 1960. First published as *Pioneers of the Modern Movement*, Faber and Faber, London, 1936.

7
Richards, J.M., *An Introduction to Modern Architecture*, Pelican Books, Harmondsworth, 1940.

8
Colquhoun, A., 'Symbolic and literal aspects of technology', *Architectural Design*, November 1962. Reprinted in *Essays in Architectural Criticism: Modern Architecture and Historical Change*, Opposition Books, MIT Press, Cambridge, Mass., 1981.

9
Kermode, F., Hollander, J., *Introduction to Modern British Literature*, The Oxford Anthology of English Literature, Oxford University Press, Oxford, 1973.

10
Olley, J., 'The Reform Club' and 'The Natural History Museum', in Cruickshank, D. (ed.), *Timeless Architecture: 1*, Architectural Press. London, 1985; Port, M.H. (ed.), *The Houses of Parliament*, Yale University Press, New Haven. 1976.

11
Gropius, W., *The New Architecture and the Bauhaus*, Faber and Faber, London, 1935.

# Environment at the threshold

8.1
Office type and environmental typology.

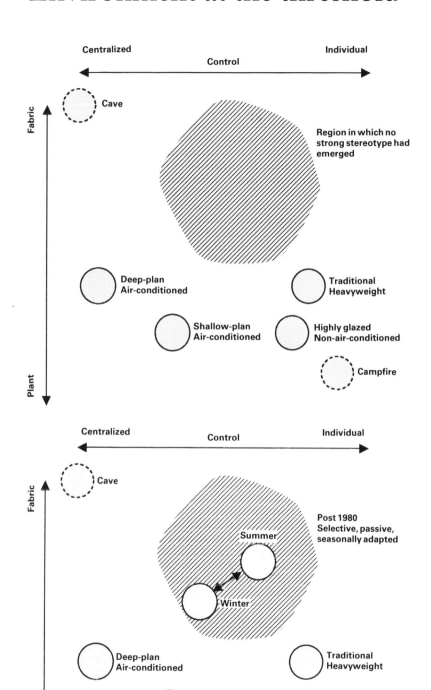

8.2
Selective office and the 'solution space'.

## Introduction

One of the most marked trends in architecture over the centuries has been that of replacing the functions of the building structure by engineering service systems. In earliest times the mass of the structure provided security and protection from climatic extremes, and openings in the structure provided light and ventilation. Over the years the function of security has been partly taken over by electronic control devices and the function of moderating climatic variation has been taken over by heating and cooling plant. Some of the functions of the window, the provision of light and ventilation, are now performed by engineering systems.

It is a matter of some debate as to whether or not this trend is a good one; it may be that it is more economic to allow the structure to perform these 'portmanteau' functions. The trend is not likely to be reversed, however, because the increased control which individual services afford over the built environment is now the norm expected by users of all building types. All the evidence points to pressure for greater control in the future.

Writing in 1971, Thomas Maver presented a lucid synopsis of the historical development of environmental design in buildings, and offered a plausible prediction of its future direction, which has been substantially borne out by the events of the mid-1970s to mid-1990s.[1] My aim, in this essay, is to present an analysis of the situation in the field as we approach the end of the twentieth century and, from this, to suggest that the potential exists for a radical transformation of both the theory and the practices of environmental design.

The process referred to by Maver, by which engineering service systems have taken over the environmental functions of the building structure, received its greatest stimulus in the Industrial Revolution. The coincidence of scientific and technological development and social transformation had, among its many consequences, a profound impact upon the design of buildings. The creation of new modes of production, new patterns of residence and the proliferation of new institutions produced new demands on the form and performance of buildings. In the present context the most significant of these was the rejection of the historical symbiosis between the naturally occurring climate and the environment within buildings. It was unacceptable for the use of a building to be restricted to certain periods of the year, or only to daylight hours. It was equally undesirable for the occupants of a building, certainly of an industrial, commercial or institutional building, to be required to devote their time and effort to its operation. The 'environmental brief' was, in the most general terms, for a building to offer an appropriate standard of comfort at the required time of day or night, or season of the year, with the minimum amount of effort on the part of the users.[2]

This transformation depended upon the achievements of the scientific revolution which, from its origins in the Renaissance, reached out, in industrial Britain and revolutionary France, to engage with the practical concerns of everyday life.[3] But, in the building field, as in many other applications, pragmatism often played a greater part than theory. As the nineteenth century progressed, environmental design was increasingly based upon general statements that established quantitative relationships between the environment and the means by which these might be achieved, as is shown by the following quotation from *Gwilt's Encyclopedia of Architecture*, 1842:

One foot of superficies of heating surface is required for every 6 feet of glass; the same for every 120 feet of wall, roof and ceiling; and an equivalent quantity for every 6 cubic feet of air withdrawn from the apartment by ventilation per minute.[4]

From this it is clear that much environmental design had an established quantitative basis well before the end of the nineteenth century. There were, however, two significant developments that occurred just as the nineteenth century closed, which were to have a fundamental effect upon the events in the twentieth century.

### The twentieth century: electricity and building science

The pioneering research into the understanding and harnessing of electricity constitutes one of the great stories of eighteenth-century science. Its practical generation and application occurred, in primitive form, in the early part of the nineteenth century. In the field of building environment, however, the most significant step towards the widespread application of electricity was made in 1879 with the virtually simultaneous invention by Thomas Edison in the USA and Joseph Swan in Britain, of the incandescent lamp. This ensured the introduction of large-scale electricity generation and the rapid exploitation of electrical power for an ever increasing number of applications in buildings, thus releasing building services from the cumbersome physical and dimensional constraints of steam power.

The other event was very different in nature, but was at least as significant in its impact on environmental design practice. This was the emergence of building science as a distinct and respectable discipline. It is difficult to be precise about the identity of the first building scientist, in the modern meaning of the term, but the achievement of Wallace Clement Sabine in transforming architectural acoustics, from its nineteenth-century reliance on often contradictory rules-of-thumb, to a secure foundation on scientific principle, may be taken to represent the changes that took place across the environmental field.[5] Shortly afterwards the importance of the new discipline was acknowledged in a number of countries by the establishment of state-financed research institutes.[6]

The advent of electrical power led to the development of numerous devices for the improved environmental servicing of buildings. Fans made mechanical ventilation convenient to control and easy to accommodate in the building structure. Compressors made the supply of cooling as simple as heating. Brought together, in the form of air conditioning, these made year-round tempering of the thermal environment a practical possibility in all buildings. The efficiency of artificial lighting was significantly increased by the development of the fluorescent lamp by George Westinghouse and GEC in 1938. It opened up the possibility of a new synthesis of the visual and thermal environments, in which mechanical services assumed the primary role in environmental control.

In the world of building science the first half of the twentieth century witnessed the establishment of the foundations of the theory of environmental comfort, in the work of building scientists such as Bedford, Dufton, Gagge, Houghten, Missenard, Vernon and Yaglou in the thermal field; of Hartridge, Hecht, Luckeish and Walsh in establishing relationships between light and vision; and of Watson, Knudsen, Hope Bagenal and Wood in acoustics.

A necessary complement to the definition of quantitative goals for environmental design is, of course, the production of calculation methods for use in design. The development of methods for calculating the heat requirements of buildings demanded the derivation of simple equations, from a basis in the theory of thermodynamics, and the empirical measurement of the thermal properties of building materials. Out of this the universally applied steady-state heat loss calculation, based on the concept of the *U-value*, was produced.

In lighting design, Harrison and Anderson's lumen method, first proposed in 1916, has assumed a level of acceptance that may be compared with the use of steady-state heat loss in thermal analysis, and the work of Waldram and Waldram placed the calculation of levels of daylight on a sound footing early in the 1920s. In acoustics, Bagenal and Wood's *Planning for Good Acoustics*, first published in 1931,[7] shows the extent to which the foundations of present-day theory were laid by this period, with its exposition of the fundamentals of room acoustics and of sound transmission, and its extensive tables of the acoustic properties of many building materials and common forms of construction.

All of this work was undertaken in the two decades between the world wars. In the postwar period the use of the technologies of environmental control passed from the realm of novelty into everyday practice and the existence of methods of calculation, everyday practice and the existence of methods of calculation, related to widely accepted, quantitatively expressed design standards, enabled the profession of environmental, or perhaps more accurately, services, consultant to assume a more significant role in the building design team. Work on the refinement of existing service systems and the invention of new technologies has continued apace, and research in environmental science has become a major activity in research institutes and universities in many countries. All of this has had an effect on the nature of the buildings that have been designed and constructed, and upon the nature of the environments they contain.

## Evolution in environmental design

In 'Types, norms and habit', I sketched out an evolutionary tale describing the development of the British office building from the end of the nineteenth century up to the 1970s. The central argument of the essay is that the theoretical and practical attractions of the combination of quantitative environmental design specifications and mechanical services systems led designers into a cul-de-sac of technological determinism, which had serious implications for the nature of the internal environment. It also risked the destruction of the association of inside and outside which was, in a profound sense, a primary generator of architectural form throughout history.

## The environmental system

In an attempt to establish a theoretical basis for a way out of this apparent dead-end, work was undertaken by Hawkes and Willey[8] on the development of a comprehensive theoretical model of the environmental system in architecture. This model described the interrelationships between energy sources – the building fabric, plant and occupants – as a network composed of flows of energy and of information. In general terms it is possible to describe the environmental structure of any building as a subset of this model. A simple distinction was drawn between two modes of environmental control, the *selective* and the *exclusive*, which reflect, in their definition, the traditional balance of fabric and plant – *selective*; and the late twentieth-century emphasis of plant over fabric – *exclusive*. The different systemic structure of each can be revealed by reference to the general model.

The other function of the model was to indicate the extent and potential of the participation of the occupant of a building in the processes of environmental control, and to reveal the relative paucity of research into the nature of user response at that time. A study of the interaction between occupants and environments in five school buildings produced valuable insights into this subject,[9] and led to the design and construction of an innovative school building at Netley in Hampshire (discussed in Part Two).

In the case of the office building, the historical typology was mapped on to a two-dimensional 'solution-space', defined in terms of the relative roles of fabric and plant along one axis and individual or centralized control along the other (Figures 8.1 and 8.2). This revealed a substantial area in which, at the time of this work, no significant designs were found.

It is clear that there has been in recent years a clear move away from the deterministic tendency of the 1960s and early 1970s in the direction of a new pluralism of approach. In order to round off my argument I will try to identify the nature and origins of these developments and to illustrate the way in which they have been applied in practice.

## Towards the new environment

To begin with the fundamental issue of the design specification, attention has been increasingly directed towards a more 'tolerant' definition of the nature of the ideal environment.[10] No longer is control within narrow, quantitatively defined limits seen as the goal, nor is absolute environmental uniformity throughout a space, or even an entire building, regarded as necessarily desirable. It is now acknowledged that a degree of temporal and spatial diversity may, in many instances, be preferable. The other development in this area is the restoration of a degree of occupant control, both collectively and individually, in the selection and maintenance of environmental conditions.

While discussing the specification as the primary generator of the design solution, in terms of the modern movement's *form follows function* model, it is essential to note that, in many environments, the tools of the trade, particularly of modern big business, make greater demands on the environmental control system than their human users. For example, the need to remove heat gains produced by the enormous electrical loads of a dealing room, overwhelms the mere provision of a humanly acceptable temperature and ventilation rate. The term 'incidental gains' is no longer adequate to describe these inputs. In those buildings where these occur, they fundamentally redefine the parameters of the equation of environmental control, and inevitably demand dependence on mechanical plant.

At the other end of the technological spectrum we are witnessing a revival of interest in the 'natural' environment. This is partly an element of the new 'tolerant' basis of design specification, and is also fuelled by the interest in 'passive' systems, which has followed from the 'energy crisis' of the 1970s. The possibility of reducing energy costs by the substitution of artificial lighting by 'free' daylight is receiving attention from researchers and designers[11] and the theory and practice of predictable and controllable natural ventilation are also developing rapidly.[12] Passive approaches to meeting the heating and cooling loads of buildings are now developing from the domestic-scale applications of the early 1980s and are being seen in designs for non-domestic buildings of many types.[13]

Moving now from the goals of environmental design to the technical means by which they may be achieved, we should note important developments in the nature of the building fabric and the systems that operate within it.

Historically, one of the primary questions in the design of the building envelope has been the size of window openings. The great treatises of Alberti, Palladio and Serlio all pay attention to this, and there was much discussion in eighteenth-century England of the necessary adjustment to Palladio's mathematically defined ratios in order to adapt them to the dimmer light of the northern latitudes. In the twentieth century the modern movement saw the potential of large areas of glass as a crucial element of the 'new architecture',[14] but this was rapidly contradicted by the move towards small areas of glass which developments in mechanical servicing permitted.

The whole question is opened-up by developments in the performance of glass and glazing systems. A glazed opening need no longer be a major source of heat loss in winter, nor of heat gain in summer. Multilayered glazing using low-emissivity coatings and, possibly, gas-filled cavities can produce thermal insulation levels which, by British standards at least, would have been considered to be good for wall and roof constructions not very long ago.

The concern of traditional thermal analysis was to calculate the rate of heat transfer through the external envelope of a building. Developments in computer simulation models have, in addition to moving on from steady-state to dynamic analysis, drawn attention to the effect of the internal fabric on the environment, particularly the effect of exposed thermal mass on the response of a building to sources of heat.

Within this new building envelope the potential of the plant is now almost infinite. Control can be applied at both the macro and micro scale, so that an individual may fine-tune his or her local environment. The operation of plant is now commonly linked to the external environment through optimum building-management systems, and distinct seasonal modes of operation are adopted. Heat recovery technology often makes a significant contribution to reducing the operating costs of a building. There is also great potential for the integration of mechanical plant and passive systems in optimizing the use of natural and artificial light, and in the reduction of ventilation heat losses through the passive

## Notes and references

1
Maver, T., *Building Services Design: A Systemic Approach to Decision-making*, RIBA Publications, London, 1971.

2
Banham, R., *The Architecture of the Well-tempered Environment*, Architectural Press, London, 1969.

3
Bernal, J.D., *Science in History*, illustrated edition, 4 vols., Penguin Books, Harmondsworth, 1969.

4
Gwilt, J., *An Encyclopedia of Architecture: Historical, Theoretical and Practical*, Longmans, Green and Co., London, 1842.

5
Sabine, W.C., 'Reverberation', in *The American Architect*, 1900. Reprinted in Hunt, F. (ed.), *Collected Papers on Acoustics*, Dover, New York, 1964.

6
Lea, F.M., *History of the Building Research Station*, HMSO, London, 1974.

7
Bagenal, H. and Wood, A., *Planning for Good Acoustics*, Methuen, London, 1931.

8
Hawkes, D. and Willey, H., 'User response in the environmental control system', in *Transactions of the Martin Centre for Architectural and Urban Studies*, vol. 2, Woodhead-Faulkner, Cambridge, 1977.

9
Haigh, D., 'User response in environmental control', in Hawkes, D. and Owers, J., *The Architecture of Energy*, Construction Press/Longman, Harlow, 1982.

10
See, for example, Wyon, D., and Cooper, I. (eds), 'Comfort and energy conservation in buildings', *Energy and Buildings*, vol. 5, no. 2, December 1982.

11
Baker, N. and Fontonyont, M., *Technical Design Guidelines for the Thermal and Daylighting Design of Non-domestic Buildings*, Commision of the European Communities, Directorate for Science, Research and Development, Brussels, 1988.

12
Baker, N., 'Passive solar ventilation preheating', in Palz, W. (ed.), *Proceedings of 1987 European Conference on Architecture*, H.S. Stephens and Associates, Bedford, 1987.

13
Commission of the European Communities, 'Working in the City', Architectural Design Competition, Commission of the European Communities, Directorate for Science, Research and Development, Brussels, 1988.

14
Le Corbusier and Jeanneret, P., '5 points d'une architecture nouvelle', *Die Form*, vol. 2, 1972.

preheating of supply air.

Returning, now, to the evolutionary analogy, suggested by my opening quotation from Maver, and the historical evidence of a close, if complex, interrelationship between developments in the science and technology of environmental control and building design practice, we are confronted by the question of what the next steps in this evolution may be.

At the most general level we seem to be moving into a period of diversity of approach, which, in terms of classical Darwinism, is more propitious than the relatively narrow concentration of the mechanically dominated vision implied by Maver's analysis. Instead of accepting a generalized conception of the environment, created and sustained by a particular interrelationship of fabric and plant, it is now possible to begin with a more complex and differentiated statement of the aims of design, and to consider a series of alternative approaches to its realization.

The effect of this is to acknowledge the differences between the environmental requirements of activities, rather than to emphasize their similarities. In the same way, the differences in the external environment at macro and micro level can be taken into account. From this we may see the restoration of the fundamental distinctions between building types, both in relation to their purpose and location, which were found in architecture before the application of numerical specifications and their complementary technologies began to assert a bland uniformity.

This is not, it must be stressed, a retrogressive proposition, an appeal to nostalgic historicism, but a recognition that there now exists a level of understanding about human environmental needs, a rich and diverse set of technologies and related tools of analysis, which offers the prospect of a new synthesis of architectural science and design practice.

The effect of this may be discerned by reference to the 'solution-space' defined by Willey (Figures 8.1 and 8.2). Since this was first plotted a number of design types have appeared in the previously unoccupied zone. We may expect the 'space' to be extensively occupied as the new possibilities are progressively explored in practice.

I see these developments presenting two significant challenges for the field of environmental research. First is the need to direct studies of user requirements towards the understanding of environmental diversity, both spatial and temporal, and of the complex perceptual and operational relationships which occur in the total environment. Second is the task of re-examining the relationship of plant and fabric. Both of these demand a major effort in the next decade if research is to keep pace with the rapidly evolving demands of practice.

# The Cambridge School and the environmental tradition

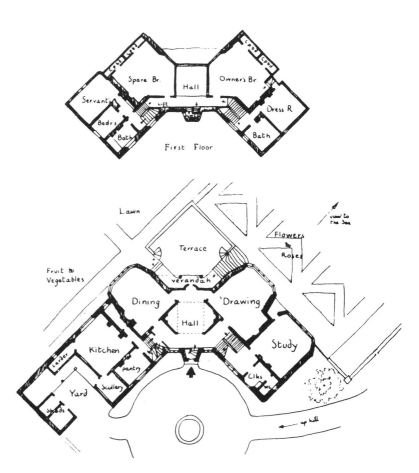

9.1
Edward Prior, The Barn, Exmouth, 1897.

9.2
Edward Prior, Home Place, Holt, Norfolk, 1905.

## Environmental origins

The school of architecture at Cambridge was founded in 1912 as a result of the efforts of the then Slade Professor of Art, Edward Schroeder Prior, who, in addition to his reputation as a historian of the gothic age, was a major figure in the arts and crafts movement in architecture.[1] Prior's buildings, such as his houses at Exmouth, 1897, and Holt, 1905, (Figures 9.1 and 9.2), were a particularly idiosyncratic variant upon the arts and crafts theme with their 'butterfly' plans. They do, however, exhibit the concern for environmental matters, which was a consistent element of the work of the whole movement. They are particularly careful in the way in which they achieve a southerly orientation for the principal rooms in order to capture the warmth of the winter sun, a kind of 'proto-passive solar design'. In his church of St Andrew's at Roker, 1907,[2] Prior demonstrated an interest in another aspect of environmental design in his use of an electrically propelled warm-air heating system (Figure 9.3).

One should not read too much into this evidence of early environmentalism, but it is interesting to note the consistent influence of environmental factors in the work of architects associated with the Cambridge School. The influence of the arts and crafts upon the modern movement was powerfully asserted by Pevsner in *Pioneers of Modern Design*,[3] and, although his argument had no environmental dimension, it is possible to see an arts and crafts connection in the plan of the Thurso House built, in Cambridge in 1932, by George Checkley who was then teaching in the school (Figure 9.4).

In his essay, 'Background and Belief',[4] Leslie Martin illustrated the house at Brampton in Cumberland that he and Sadie Speight designed in 1937. He described the house as adopting the English free school (or arts and crafts) method of 'planning around use, site and aspect'. This reference to aspect, to the southerly orientation of the principal rooms of the house, connects his work back to the tradition of Prior. It also prefigures the engagement with environmental matters that may be seen to run through his work, and that of his many associates, in the prolific period of practice following his move to Cambridge in 1956 as the first holder of the university's Chair of Architecture.

The importance of orientation may be seen in Martin's buildings of a larger scale, in the plans of College Hall at Leicester, designed with Trevor Dannatt and completed in 1959, and Harvey Court, designed with Colin St John Wilson for Gonville and Caius College at Cambridge and completed in 1962 (Figure 9.5). The group of libraries at Manor Road, Oxford, also designed with Wilson and completed in 1964 (Figure 9.6), have a series of roof-lit reading rooms in which the design of the rooflights achieves a carefully

9.3
Edward Prior, St Andrew's Church
Roker, 1907.

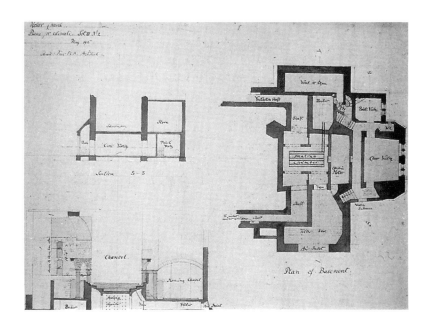

9.4
George Checkley, Thurso House,
Cambridge, 1932.

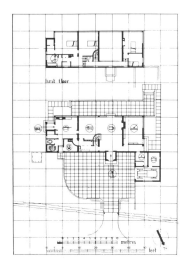

calculated balance between the provision of good levels of natural light and the avoidance of overheating in summer.

The 1970 extension to Kettle's Yard in Cambridge, designed by Martin and David Owers to house Jim Ede's collection of twentieth-century art, demonstrates another approach to the control of daylight in which a cross-section of great simplicity is manipulated to produce a result that is simultaneously functional and poetic (Figure 9.7). The problem of the large-scale art museum led Martin and Ivor Richards, at the Gulbenkian Museum of Contemporary Art in Lisbon, 1984, to a further variation on the theme of the rooflight. As at the Oxford libraries this building, with its north-facing, stepped rooflights and planted terraces, is concerned with the balance between daylight and the thermal environment, but in this case in a more challenging climate (Figure 9.8).

The design of auditoria, and particularly of spaces for the performance of music, is a theme, with variations, which runs through Martin's work from the Royal Festival Hall of 1951 to the Glasgow Royal Concert Hall in the 1980s. In these it is possible to observe the effects of developing theory in acoustics through the transformation of the 'shoebox' plan of the Festival Hall into the more elaborate 'surround-sound' configuration at Glasgow.

My intention in drawing attention to the environmental strand which runs through these projects is to show that these concerns were already in the background to the research that has evolved in the Cambridge School since the mid-1960s – that practice may precede, as well as follow from, research. In this connection I am attracted by Bruno Zevi's contention[5] that, when Arnold Schoenberg consolidated his freely created new musical language through its codification in the 12-tone system, his architectural contemporaries, such as Voysey and Mackintosh, Horta and Olbrich, Sullivan and Gaudí, Le Corbusier, Hugo Häring and Mendelsohn, failed to make a similar step – to establish rules. In other words, that they failed to support the developments of their practice by research. These buildings also remind us that, however important it may be to study in detail specific aspects of the performance and behaviour of buildings, the ultimate issue in architecture is one of synthesis in which delicate balances must be sought between often contradictory requirements.

In recent years questions of environment and energy have been on the agenda of many architects. It is notable, however, that some of the most important contributions to the question of synthesis, of combining new technical understanding with the constant and continuing concerns of architecture, have been made by architects with connections with the Cambridge School. In the work of, for instance, Colin St John Wilson, Edward Cullinan, Richard Mac-Cormac, David Lea, Feilden Clegg, Short Ford and Brenda and Robert Vale, the line may be seen to continue in addressing the redefined environmental issues of the end of the century.

## Modes of environmental control

In attempting to establish some clarity and structure in the understanding of the issues and potential of the environmental theme in architecture, I proposed, in 'Building shape and energy use', a simple distinction, between two modes of environmental control – the 'selective' and the 'exclusive'. This argued the virtues, with respect to environmental quality and energy-saving, of 'Selective' designs, which use the form and fabric of the building envelope as a filter of the external environment. In combination with the idea of user control of envelope, plant and systems, this approach can produce designs that are energy-saving, environmentally sound and architecturally rich.

The alternative strategy of the 'exclusive' is characterized as achieving energy efficiency through the establishment of a relationship between building form and mechanical and electrical service systems in which the environment is predominantly artificial, control wholly automatic and centralized, and in which the entire building depends upon the continuous consumption of energy – no energy, no environment!

Upon reflection, this categorization, while it describes a specific and important distinction, fails to address the nature of the vast and uncharted bulk of buildings in which there is little or no conscious engagement with environmental design. These may be said to inhabit a third category, the 'pragmatic' mode. To relate this to the 'selective' and 'exclusive' modes it may be amusing, and helpful, to

9.5
Leslie Martin and Colin St J Wilson, Harvey Court, Gonville and Caius College, Cambridge, 1962.

9.6
Leslie Martin and Colin St J Wilson, Manor Road Libraries, Oxford, 1964.

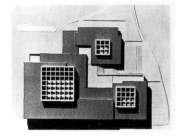

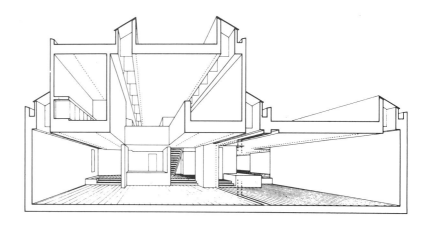

9.7
Leslie Martin and David Owers, Kettle's
Yard, Cambridge, 1970.

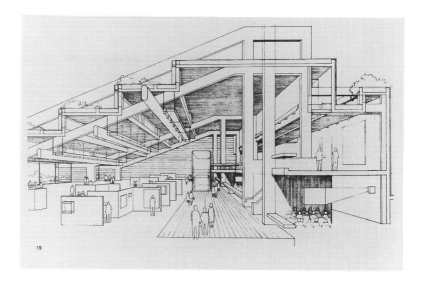

9.8
Leslie Martin and Ivor Richards,
Gulbenkian Museum of Contemporary
Art, Lisbon, 1984.

borrow an idea from city planning, Ebenezer Howard's 'three magnets' diagram, and propose the 'three magnets of environment' (Figure 9.9).

## Typology and environmental design

In classical passive solar design there is a standard typology of 'direct gain', 'sun-space', 'Trombe wall' and 'roof collector' systems of collection of solar heat gain. This is useful as a representation of technical options, but it hardly begins to address the more complex demands of architectural design.

For many years I have been interested in the potential of the idea of type as a basis for environmental design, beginning with the essay, 'Type, norms and habit in environmental design', first published in 1976. That essay was conceived very much under the influence of Alan Colquhoun's 'Typology and design method',[6] in which he argued that type transcends the limitations of the reductivist propositions of the design method school of the 1960s by embracing functional and symbolic concerns. My argument is that type offers the possibility of translating the results of technically-based research into a form that renders them accessible to designers.

As an indication of the nature of an environmental typology, I propose a provisional structure for a 'selective typology' (Figure 9.10). This takes as its starting point the classical work of Leslie Martin and Lionel March on the distinction between courts and pavilions.[7] It also incorporates Nick Baker's distinction, in his work on the 'LT' method of energy analysis, between 'passive' and 'non-passive' zones, in which the passive zone is defined as extending 6 metres from the perimeter of a building.[8]

The transformation in environmental conditions and energy performance that follows from glazing over a courtyard is now well established and understood. It is still all too common, however, to encounter designs in practice that fail to recognize the parameters within which effective 'selective' performance may be achieved and which, as a consequence, revert to environmental pragmatism. The pavilion, when applied to certain functions, is appropriate for the achievement of good 'selective' performance. If its long axis lies east–west, direct-gain, sun-space or Trombe-wall techniques can be effectively exploited. In this way a further category is added to the typology.

These 'primitives', as Lionel March once described them, 'animals of architecture', are, of course, unlike most viable buildings. They are devoid of the complex layerings of function, association and symbol which, as Colquhoun's essay reminds us, are essential to the transformation of mere form into the essence of architecture. Their value is, I suggest, that they offer a repertoire of possibilities upon which these complex decisions and choices may be founded. All of the configurations illustrated in the simple 'selective typology' chart exhibit the properties and potential of the 'selective' mode. I contend that the 'selective' mode is itself based upon the essential association of external and internal environments which has fundamentally informed the creation of architecture throughout its history. As Louis Kahn so memorably observed, 'the sun never knew how great it is until it struck the side of a building' (p. 72).

The next step is to extend the taxonomy by developing further combinations and, then, to produce a commentary, both quantitative, through mathematical modelling exercises – parametric studies as they are now called – and qualitative so that it may inform the process of selection in design. In doing this the relation of form and function would be examined, not in the simplistic, deterministic sense of the slogan 'form follows function', but through a more specific engagement with the particular and profound implications of the demands of dwellings, schools, offices, hospitals, or whatever, in defining the objectives of environmental design and, hence, of energy analysis.

## The energy of cities

A recurrent concern in the Cambridge School's environmetal work has been to move from the study of the individual building to that of the city. In our 1978 essay on glazed courtyards,[9] Richard MacCormac and I suggested the possibility of a revival of the nineteenth-century vision of a network of arcades running through the entire urban fabric providing a protected environment for social discourse and exchange in parallel to the open system of streets. In its modern manifestation, such a structure would also bestow the further benefit of reducing the energy needs of the city.

Koen Steemers' studies of the relationship between the form of the central urban block and its energy needs continues this line of work.[10] This shows how the overshadowing of adjacent buildings in dense city centres affects levels of natural light and the availability of incident solar radiation in either, positively, contributing to winter heating or, negatively, producing summertime overheating. The work shows that, with careful design, the principles of 'selective' design are valid in designing buildings for the whole range of uses found in the centre of the modern city.

In the past 25 years the environmental agenda of architecture, in both practice and research, has undergone a radical transformation. The 'energy crisis' of the early 1970s provoked a fundamental change in which, mainly through improvements in the requirements of building regulations, all buildings are to some extent more energy efficient and in which the best of conventional practice has

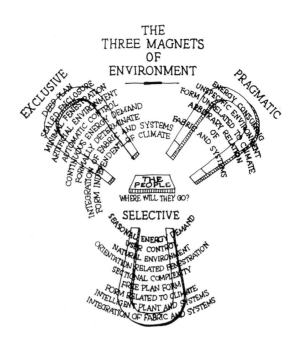

THE
THREE MAGNETS
OF
ENVIRONMENT

assimilated the products of research to achieve still better performance. In many cases this is done by displacing the consumption of delivered energy by carefully designing the form and fabric of the building to reduce demand and to garner the benefits of ambient energy, by the adoption of a 'selective' approach.

There is, however, a need to raise higher the stakes of both practice and research. It has been observed[11] that there is, in most of the highly populated areas of the world, many times more ambient energy striking the external envelopes of buildings, in the form of sun and wind, than they consume in sustaining the functions which they house and in the maintenance of a comfortable environment. Yet only a small fraction of that energy is tapped by even the best solar buildings. If a greater conversion rate could be achieved the prospect begins to emerge of buildings that are producers rather than consumers of energy. The implications of this for the future of the city are remarkable.

If we turn to Johann Heinrich von Thünen's classic diagram of the 'isolated state' (Figure 9.11), we may note that, after horticulture and dairy farming, sylviculture lies closest to the central city. This is because forest products were the city's energy source and their availability at low cost was essential to the economy of the whole state. How different is the modern pragmatic city, where even the most recent buildings frequently consume vast quantities of non-renewable fuel to reject the ambient energy which impinges upon them. The energy hinterland of this city is so dispersed that it could not be encompassed by von Thünen's diagram. A city such as London is supported by a network of power stations located as far

9.10
A 'selective' typology.

9.11
Johann Heinrich Von Thünen, 'The isolated state'.

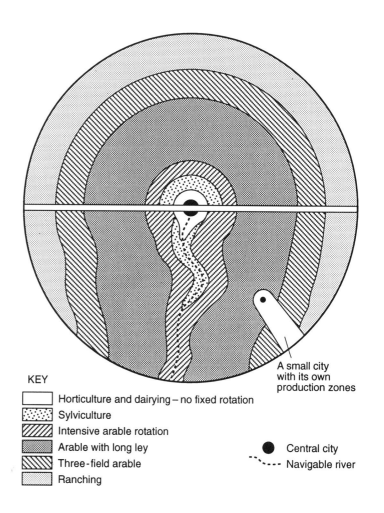

A small city with its own production zones

KEY

☐ Horticulture and dairying – no fixed rotation
▨ Sylviculture
▨ Intensive arable rotation
▨ Arable with long ley
▨ Three-field arable
▨ Ranching

● Central city
‑‑‑‑ Navigable river

away as the north of England, in the case of traditional coal-burning plant, and around the coastline, in the case of the nuclear plant. Gas and oil are piped in from the North Sea and further afield. This is a system of great complexity and fraught with risk and danger.

The city that produces all of the energy it needs for its buildings and the urban infrastructure is, of course, only a vision. To take the first steps towards its realization would transform the agenda for research and practice in architecture more radically than any idea since the advent of the modern movement.

## Notes and references

1
Hawkes, D., 'The Cambridge School: tradition, research and practice', *Architectural Review*, May 1984.

2
Hawkes, D., 'St Andrew's, Roker' in Cruickshank, D. (ed.), *Timeless Architecture: 1*, Architectural Press, London, 1985.

3
Pevsner, N., *Pioneers of Modern Design*, Penguin Books, Harmondsworth, 1960.

4
Martin, L, 'Background and belief', in *Buildings and Projects, 1935–1985*, Cambridge University Press, Cambridge, 1986.

5
Zevi, B., 'Architecture versus historic criticism', in *RIBA Transactions 5*, Royal Institute of British Architects, London, 1984.

6
Colquhoun, A., 'Typology and design method', *Arena*, June 1967. Reprinted in *Essays in Architectural Criticism*, MIT Press, Cambridge, Mass., 1981.

7
Martin, L. and March, L., 'Built form and land use', *Cambridge Research*, April 1966.

8
Baker, N., 'The LT method, version 2.0', Cambridge Architectural Research Ltd. and the Martin Centre for Architectural and Urban Studies, Cambridge, undated.

9
Hawkes, D. and MacCormac, R., 'Office form and energy use', *RIBA Journal*, June 1978.

10
Steemers, K., Baker, N. and Hawkes, D., *Energy Use and Development*. Proceedings of the second European conference on architecture. Kluwer, Dordrecht, 1990.

11
Anderson, B., *Solar Building Architecture*, MIT Press, Cambridge, Mass., 1990.

# Part Two

# Design

# 10 Wallasey School: pioneer of solar design

ARCHITECT: EMSLIE A. MORGAN

St George's School at Wallasey on the Wirral peninsula is one of the seminal buildings in the development of what is now known as passive solar design. Its clear-cut form, with a steeply sloping monopitch roof rising from a virtually windowless north façade to the top of the 9 m-high solar wall, is a direct expression of the fundamental principles in the exploitation of solar gain to heat a building.[1,2] It was not, however, a product of the upsurge of interest in energy-saving design which followed the so-called energy crisis of the early 1970s. Its designer was the assistant borough architect of Wallasey, Emslie A. Morgan, and it was completed in 1961. There was nothing in Morgan's earlier work which in any way hinted at what he went on to produce at St George's. And, because he died in 1964, the building has no direct progeny. It stands as a magnificent isolated specimen, detached from any rational process of architectural evolution, but anticipating future developments (Figure 10.1).

In the circumstances, it is not surprising that the building has accumulated a body of myths and half truths which conspire to obscure its true nature, its vices and virtues. In this essay, an attempt is made to present a straightforward and accurate description of the building as it was constructed and to offer an appraisal of its performance since it first opened its doors.

The school was constructed as an annexe to a building completed in 1954. The site plan is dated July 1957 and the ⅛ in-scale working drawings were produced in 1958 with large scale drawings following in 1959. The plan form of the earlier 1955 building is typical of school design practice in Britain in this period, with narrow section, daylit blocks of rooms arranged orthogonally around an open courtyard and protected paved areas. The cranked, linear plan of the annexe, as shown on the 1957 site plan, clearly indicates that a radically different set of ideas were in play.

The ground-floor plan, shows the diagrammatic clarity of the arrangement with a sequence of ground-floor classrooms to the south of the main corridor, which links the main entrance and assembly hall at the west to a slightly disconnected block to the east. This contains the gymnasium at ground level and the woodwork and metalwork rooms at first floor above the changing rooms. The first floor of the classroom block has three further classrooms and the library, art room and science laboratory. These extend the full width of the building and are approached by staircases contained within the section, avoiding the need to duplicate the corridor at the upper level (Figures 10.2–10.4).

When superimposed onto this plan, the cross-section through the classroom block gives the clearest expression of the way in which Morgan's concern to exploit the heating effects of solar gain influenced the form of the building. The massive construction of the monopitch roof, the north façade and the floor slabs, combined

10.1
North elevation.

10.2
Cross-section.

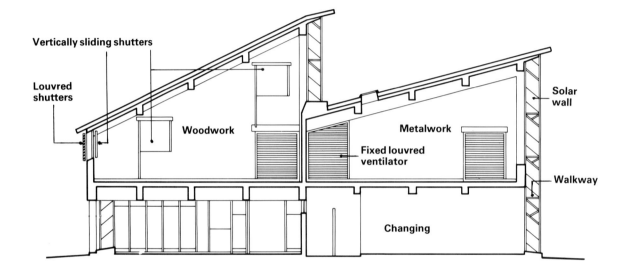

Vertically sliding shutters

Louvred
shutters

Woodwork

Metalwork

Solar
wall

Fixed louvred
ventilator

Walkway

Changing

with the thick external insulation accentuate the transparency of the tall 'solar wall' of the south façade. This standard diagram is ingeniously adapted to deal with the different requirements of the assembly hall and the double-banked planning of the woodwork and metalwork rooms. A flat roof is used over the gymnasium, presumably dictated by the demands of indoor sports, but the essential features of the standard section, in terms of construction and the use of the solar wall, are maintained.

A remarkable series of notebooks compiled by Morgan have survived.[3] They record his apparently self-tutored exploration of the fundamentals of thermodynamics, the properties of building materials and of aspects of building science. These suggest that the form of the building owed more to the systemic application of scientific principle than to any conscious reference to precedent. It is hardly surprising, therefore, that an intelligent consideration of the issues involved in deriving maximum benefit from solar gain should lead him to an overall form that is similar to many subsequent passive solar designs. But, when we move on to examine the detailed design of the building, it becomes clear that Morgan was using his newly acquired technical understanding to make, and eventually construct, entirely novel propositions about the nature of the environment in the building and the means by which it could be controlled.

The fundamental assumption in the design of the building was that, if the level of thermal insulation and disposition of thermal mass could be correctly organized, it should be possible to maintain an acceptable internal temperature throughout the heating season by a combination of solar gain, the heat produced by the metabolic processes of the occupants and the heat output of the electric lighting installation. It should also be possible to avoid unacceptably high summer temperatures.

The cross-section through the classroom block shows how Morgan set about bringing all the variables of this architectural equation into a harmonious relationship. The concrete and brick structure is encased in 125 mm of insulation with an outer weatherproof protection of bituminous felt. The ground floor slab has no edge insulation, but there is a 100 mm layer of lightweight concrete over the 150 mm structural slab. The soffits of the roof and first-floor slabs are left exposed.

The solar wall is over 8 m high and is 600 mm deep between its inner and outer surfaces. It is constructed of a light steel frame on a 1050 mm module, stiffened by a system of diagonal braces, which also support catwalks allowing access along the entire length of the void. The outer skin is single-glazed in relatively small panes of clear glass (1050 × 600 mm), but the design of the inner surface is much more elaborate.

Here, both clear and obscured glass are used. All of the visible

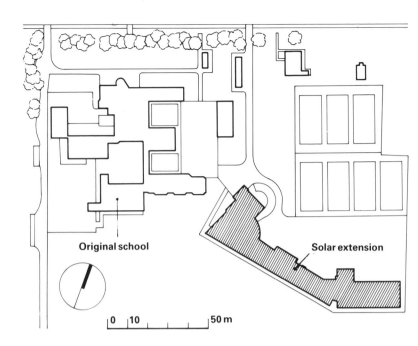

10.3
Site plan.

Original school

Solar extension

0  10                    50 m

10.4
Ground- and first-floor plans.

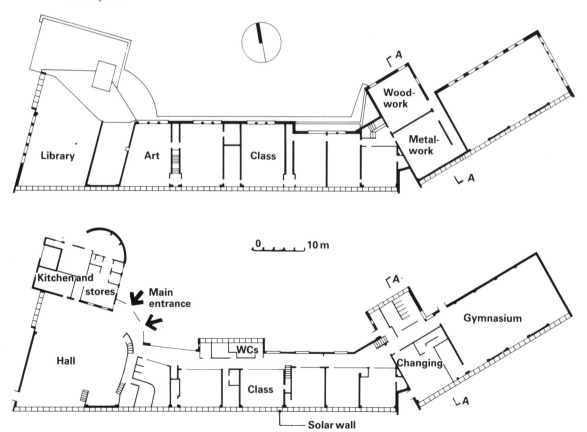

A

Wood-work

Metal-work

Library

Art

Class

0          10 m

Kitchen and stores

Main entrance

A

Gymnasium

Hall

WCs

Changing

Class

A

Solar wall

122 | The Environmental Tradition

glazing except for the lowest panels on each floor is obscured glass; the idea being that by diffusing the solar radiation it would be more evenly distributed over the surfaces of the rooms. The lowest panels and those covered by a series of pinboards have clear glass (Figure 10.5).

The pinboards are designed to be reversed according to the season of the year. One side has an aluminium-sheet face, which is directed outwards in the summer to reflect back unwanted solar gain. The other face, painted black, is intended to absorb winter radiation, and hence add to the quantity of heat that the wall will collect.

In addition to these features each room has clear-glazed opening lights of an extremely ingenious design, two to each classroom, with other rooms having more or fewer, depending on their size and function. These windows are horizontally pivoted. When the window is positioned with its top frame in the outer plane of the wall, the opening is completely sealed. If it is in the reverse position, that is with the bottom rail to the outside, controlled ventilation is achieved through fixed louvres at head and sill within the thickness of the wall, but the opening is both weather and burglar proof. Finally, it is possible for the window to be tilted further to provide increased ventilation.

Beneath each of the openable windows is the radiator supplied from the plant room in the service block to the north of the assembly hall. This heating system was installed as a precaution against the failure of the design. In fact the system has rarely been used, but despite many myths it remains operational and is used from time to time, such as during power cuts when the crucial heat from artificial lighting is not available.

In spite of Morgan's prudence in installing a conventional heating system the building has operated substantially in the manner in which he intended. An acceptable thermal environment is provided entirely by the heat produced by the occupants, the artificial lighting and the solar wall. Research has now produced detailed data which show the relative contributions from each of these sources and how they vary throughout the year. Figure 10.6 summarizes these for the period between January 1969 and July 1970. This shows that, as expected, the heat produced by the occupants varies relatively little since it is determined by the number of people present. On the other hand the contribution from artificial lighting is seasonally dependent, being at its maximum in the winter months and falling away in the summer. This correlates broadly with both a need for supplementary light and, crucially in this building, for heat in winter. Solar heat also shows a seasonal variation but it should be noted that there is a relative consistency for all but the central winter months. What is perhaps most surprising about these data is the extent to which the solar wall contributes to the heating requirement, even in the winter months of December, January and February.

**Comfort temperatures**

Figure 10.7 sets out the mean hourly air temperatures achieved during the school days for each month from January 1969 to July 1970. These show that generally the winter temperatures were comfortable with the exception of February 1969 and January 1970. Air temperature alone does not, however, determine thermal comfort. Morgan fully appreciated this and claimed in his patent application[4] that the design would achieve surface temperatures above air temperature. If this was the case, then the effects of these occurrences of low air temperatures would be mitigated. Unfortunately the research shows that the surface temperatures are generally below that of the air by a small amount, showing that Morgan's predictions were in this respect in error.

10.5
Classroom interior.

Examination of the summer temperatures in the building shows that the building is successful in avoiding unacceptable overheating. The temperatures of over 23°C in July 1969 occurred when the ambient temperature was 22.4°C. An inside-outside difference of less than 2°C in these conditions is well within acceptable limits.

### Solar wall refinements

In addition to the standard elements which apply directly to the main classroom areas, the solar wall has a number of other ingenious features. In the main block there are three positions at which a mass of masonry stands behind the wall. The largest of these is presented by the flank wall of the stage in the assembly hall. The others occur where the two internal staircases run across the plan above ground-floor store rooms. At these positions the inner glass skin is omitted and replaced by a system of hinged shutters. These are painted white on one side and clad in aluminium on the other. In the open position the aluminium surfaces reflect solar radiation on to the black painted masonry. When the shutters are closed they cover the masonry and their white face reflects the radiation back through the glass. The idea is that the shutters will be fixed open in the winter, to maximize the amount of solar gain collected, and closed in summer to help prevent overheating. Morgan originally intended that the shutters should be thermostatically operated in response to the outside temperature but this proved impractical and expensive at the time. The tremendous developments in computerized building control systems which have occurred in recent years might perhaps make such an arrangement feasible now. The shutter system is also used in the gymnasium, where panels of brickwork are used to fill in two of the five structural bays.

The opening lights in the solar wall are only the beginning of the ventilation system in the building. In the ground-floor classrooms cross-ventilation is achieved through high-level opening lights in the corridor partition, very much in the manner of many traditional corridor-plan school buildings. However, at the first-floor level Morgan once again exercised his ingenuity by installing louvred ventilators in the north-facing wall covered by hinged, insulation shutters. These permit cross-ventilation, but avoid the problems of heat loss which north-facing windows could have produced. Devices of this kind are also used in the assembly hall, gymnasium, and woodwork and metalwork rooms. In these cases, they are usually located at high level and operated by mechanical linkages.

From the beginning of its life the standard of ventilation in the building has been criticized. Writing in 1969 Manning stated '. . . there is a variety of smells throughout the school. These include food in the entrance hall and dining room and leather and sweat in the gym'.[5] This question has been the subject of detailed investigation by Davies and Davies.[6] They have compared the responses of children and teachers to environmental conditions in the solar annexe and the conventional original school building. Their results confirm that there are problems with the ventilation system during winter and summer. In summer it is difficult to achieve an adequate rate of air movement so that on warm days the building is considered uncomfortable, even though Davies' thermal monitoring suggests that the temperature is not unacceptably high. Special problems are experienced in summer in the metalwork room, where heat-producing processes are carried out, and in the gymnasium. There is evidence that there is often a conflict between achieving adequate summer ventilation, which requires full opening of the windows and louvred ventilators, and the admission of unwanted noise from other parts of the building, particularly between the ground-floor classrooms and the corridor. In winter the problem is that ventilation is only achieved at the cost of rapidly reducing the temperature.

Thermal comfort in the summer is often associated with high levels of ventilation and hence of perceptible air movement. Work in a group of schools in Essex showed that teachers consistently opened the windows to their fullest extent, and were dissatisfied with buildings in which the opportunity to do this was restricted.[7] The limited areas of openable window in the Wallasey building almost certainly result in both physical and psychological shortcomings. The answer appears to lie in increasing the openable area, which would improve the rate of air movement and its distribution in the room, thus avoiding the risk of areas of stagnant air.

In winter the problem is almost certainly due to the fact that a heating system that relies on solar gain, electric lighting and occupancy heat gains is incapable of responding to the reduction in temperature due to ventilation in the way in which a conventional heating system can. It is inherently impossible for it to deliver more heat upon demand. One of the recent developments in the theory and practice of passive solar design has been to appreciate the benefits for both energy savings and comfort of using solar gains to preheat incoming ventilation air.[8] If the void in the Wallasey solar wall had been used as a channel to draw air into the building it is likely that adequate winter ventilation could have been achieved without a serious thermal penalty.

The large areas of glass in the solar wall, at first sight, appear to ensure a high level of daylight in the building. However, studies show that the building falls short of the official standards in force at the time it was designed.[9] This is due to the extensive obstruction of the glazing by the pinboards, the reduction of transmission through the diffusing glass and the obstruction presented by the structure of the solar wall. Lighting level alone is not the basis of good lighting design. But a room with a relatively uniform distribution of light is generally preferable to one with extreme variations of level. In these terms this building is quite successful. Morgan's concern to diffuse solar heat gain has a similar effect on the visible part of the spectrum.

In a building in which artificial lighting is regarded as an essential element of the heating system, it could be argued that a limitation of natural lighting levels is sensible. The 1954 school standards, as all conventional daylighting criteria, were intended to produce buildings which are daylit throughout the year. At Wallasey this was clearly unnecessary and it is interesting to note that the use of artificial lighting as shown in Figure 10.6 is limited to the winter months. It is possible that this was intended by Morgan.

Another important aspect of lighting design is the avoidance of glare. Carter has calculated the Glare Index for the solar wall, a technique which did not exist when the school was designed, and has found that it exceeds the maximum level now recommended for classrooms. But, because it is unusual for pupils and staff to spend much time looking directly at the solar wall, this is not, in practice, a serious problem.

It is clear from the results of the painstaking research undertaken over many years that the environment in the Wallasey school has a number of shortcomings, perhaps most seriously its ventilation system. In comparison with the adjacent conventional building, however, little overall difference was found. The solar school was criticized on the grounds of ventilation and for the limitation of view through the predominantly obscured glazing. On the other hand it was considered warmer and, in general, more comfortable.

When the radical nature of Morgan's design is considered, and his boldness in striking out into this uncharted territory armed only with his self-acquired knowledge, the achievement is remarkable. In his patent specification Morgan declared his aim to be

the conception of heating the useful accommodation of a building solely by heat of radiation emanating from the sun alone or from the sun and one or more sources of artificial illumination . . .

The scientific data and the experience of a quarter of a century of continuous use demonstrate that he was extremely successful in transforming abstract theory into concrete reality. The building has acknowledged shortcomings, but these are not so serious as to inhibit its use unduly.

The most fundamental principle of passive solar design is the appreciation of the benefits of a southerly orientation. In the British temperate climate a south-facing glazed wall can, if carefully designed, produce a net heat gain over the whole of the heating

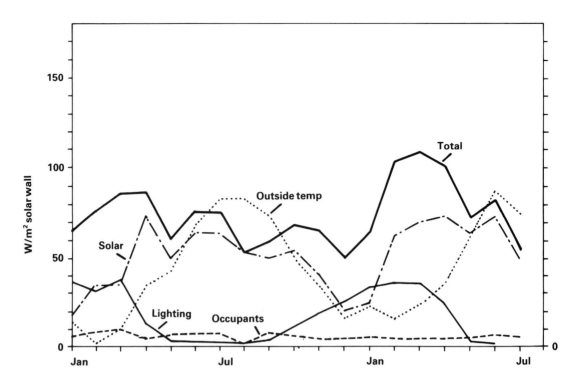

10.6
Energy inputs and ambient temperature.

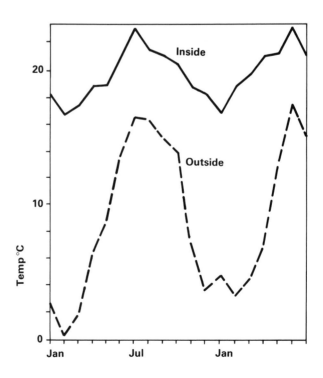

10.7
Ambient and internal daily mean
temperatures.

## Notes and references

1
Dr M. Davies of the University of Liverpool published a group of papers describing the performance of the Wallasey School in considerable detail in the journal *Energy Research* in 1987.

2
Banham, R., *The Architecture of the Well-tempered Environment*, Architectural Press, London. 1969.

3
These books are discussed in some detail by M.G. Davies in the second of his series of papers in *Energy Research*, reference No. 1.

4
Morgan applied for a patent on 6 April 1961 and the complete specification was published on 16 March 1966 as 'Improvements in solar heated buildings', UK Patent Specification 1 022 411.

5
Manning, P., 'St George's School, Wallasey: an evaluation of a solar heated building', *Architects' Journal*, 25 June 1969.

6
Davies, A.D.M. and Davies, M.G., 'User reaction to the thermal environment: the attitudes of teachers and children to St George's School, Wallasey', *Building Science*, 1971.

7
Haigh, D. 'User response in environmental control', in Hawkes, D. and Owers, J. (eds), *The Architecture of Energy*, Construction Press/Longman, Harlow, 1981.

8
Baker, N., 'The use of passive solar gains for the pre-heating of ventilation air in houses'. Report to Energy Technology Support Unit (ETSU), Harwell, 1985.

9
Carter, D.J., 'A study of the lighting of the Wallasey School'. *Energy Research*, to be published.

10
Scott, G., *The Architecture of Humanism*. Constable and Co., London, 1914.

season. In other words the gains from solar radiation exceed the losses due to conduction. St George's School, as it will continue to be known in the literature of passive solar design, stands as a monument to that principle.

In its architectural expression it is an extremely literal analogue of the physical principles which it embodies, although the scale, proportion and rhythm of the solar wall produce a result which is more than merely utilitarian. Nowadays such directness of technical expression is perhaps out of fashion. But it would be a serious error if the technical principles embodied in this building were to be associated only with a particular stylistic dogma.

In 1914 Geoffrey Scott wrote, 'The relation of construction to design is the fundamental problem of architectural aesthetics . . .'[10] If we extend the definition of construction to embrace the whole of building technology we have the starting point for a crucial enterprise in present day theory and practice, the reconciliation of rich, formal and cultural preoccupations with the wealth of technical knowledge and material which the application of science has brought to architecture. This is a difficult task. But the achievement of a pioneer like Emslie Morgan can continue to assist in the further development of the art to which he contributed so much by conceiving and realising this remarkable building.

# 11     Netley Abbey Infants' School

ARCHITECT: HAMPSHIRE COUNTY COUNCIL

Ever since the Education Act of 1870 the nature of the physical environment has been one of the major themes in school building design in Britain. In 1874, E.R. Robson, the first chief architect of the London School Board, published his book *School Architecture*.[1] This served as the principal guide for the design of schools until the first decade of the twentieth century but, as schools followed the growing population into the new suburbs, and as educational practices evolved, a new view was required. This was provided in 1902 by Felix Clays' *Modern School Building*[2] in which the transformation of the school building from an urban to a suburban type was emphatically confirmed.

As the ideas of the modern movement began to find a place in Britain, school buildings were a ready-made vehicle for the expression of the abundant provision of 'light, space and air'. In the postwar years, stimulated by the vision of R.A. Butler's Education Act of 1944, environmental concerns acquired the additional 'authority' of explicit quantitative statements of requirements, most significantly for their implications for designs, in the introduction of minimum daylight factor standards for teaching rooms. The combination of these concerns with the widespread use of system building established the broad outlines of British schools for almost a quarter of a century.

In the 1970s the longer-term consequences of this approach came home to roost. As the cultural and political pendulum swung towards a preference for diversity over uniformity, and individuality over standardization, the technical shortcomings of the system-built schools became apparent and maintenance costs began to mount. At the same time the so-called 'energy crisis' introduced a critical new parameter into the equation of environmental design.

The effect of this transformation in the underlying concerns of schools' architects has not been more strongly revealed than in the work of Hampshire County Council's Architect's Department. In this body of work, Netley Abbey Infants' School, completed in 1984, occupies a special place. It is the embodiment of a process of research and development, of collaboration between a design office and academic research, that has produced a level of technical speculation and innovation in design which would not normally be possible. It has provided the research collaborators with a rare opportunity to see their theoretical ideas translated into built reality (Figures 11.1–11.4).

During the 1970s, work was carried out at the Martin Centre in the department of architecture at Cambridge to develop a conceptual model of the 'environmental system' in architecture (summarized in 'The theoretical basis of comfort in "selective" environments'). Apart from its general utility in providing a theoretical structure for an aspect of design that had previously been conducted almost totally pragmatically, the model revealed

11.1
Interior of conservatory.

131 | Netley Abbey Infants' School

the extent to which the voluntary responses of the occupants of buildings could, and perhaps should, play a role in the processes of environmental control.

When Hampshire proposed a collaboration with the Martin Centre in developing an approach to the design of low-energy schools, it was quickly agreed that the user should play a central role. Arising from the previous research, a basic distinction was drawn between two alternative 'modes' of environmental control, the 'exclusive' and the 'selective'.

A dialogue was established between researchers at the Martin Centre and members of Hampshire Architect's Department. In the first instance the results of the survey of Essex schools[3] were translated into a generic cross-section. This indicated the difference between winter and summer modes of operation. It also demonstrated a fundamental distinction between two levels of environmental provision: the precisely controlled environment required by the sedentary activities of classroom teaching and the more loosely controlled conditions that are acceptable, even desirable, for many of the other activities which form a major part of the everyday life of a primary school.

The first detailed application of these principles in a thoroughly worked-out design was in a project for a school at Locksheath.[4] In this the generic principles were adapted to the specific circumstances of a site and a brief. The project was the victim of cuts in Hampshire's building programme but the same designers and consultants were shortly afterwards given the opportunity to work together on the design and construction of Netley Abbey Infants' School.

The new school replaced two Victorian buildings which, were situated on small sites and supplemented by the familiar clutter of temporary classrooms. The site is on the southeastern boundary of the grounds of the existing Scola system-built junior school. The brief required accommodation for children, in seven class groups, with shared spaces, administration and kitchen.

The plan consists of a principal rectangular block containing six of the class spaces and the hall. The main entrance, administration, kitchen and caretaker's accommodation are contained in a block that projects from the northwest face, and the seventh classroom and the music room are housed in wings that project from the southeast façade and which serve to define two garden areas (Figure 11.5).

The organizational, social and environmental focus of the design is the conservatory, which runs the length of the southeast façade. The children enter directly into this from the gardens when they arrive in the morning; it is their route from classroom to classroom and to the music room, hall and resources area. The main entrance is principally for adults, staff and visitors, and gives access to a small

11.2
Classroom interior.

134 | The Environmental Tradition

atrium, which serves as a focus to this adult world and provides additional natural light to the main hall.

The 'selective' approach to environmental control has two principal goals: to make maximum use of the naturally occurring climate in daylighting, ventilation and space heating and to permit the users to exercise the maximum degree of control over the selection of environmental conditions. The main elements of the approach, as they are incorporated into the Netley school, are summarized in the diagrams. This is, in broad outline, very similar to the principles established in the generic sections. The design as actually implemented required, however, a great deal of development and innovation (Figure 11.6).

In a building such as this the problem is to adapt its operation to the conditions that exist at different times of the year. In the heating season the conservatory plays a major role in the energy balance of the building. It provides additional thermal resistance to the south wall, thus reducing heat loss. In addition, the solar gains, even on a cloudy day, increase its temperature and further reduce heat loss. The heat losses from the heated classrooms further raise the conservatory temperature and help it to provide an acceptable 'intermediate' environment. The class spaces have individual warm air heaters. These are located at an upper level in the conservatory, from where they can draw fresh air, which is preheated by the combined effects of solar gains and heat losses from the heated spaces. The north-facing louvres in the classrooms remain closed in this season and all necessary fresh air enters through the conservatory. Each class space has its own controls operated by the occupants who may, therefore, exercise individual control over each space. The choices concern the room temperature, by a control marked 'warmer/cooler', and ventilation, which is achieved by a button marked 'fresh-air', which switches from a full recirculation mode to a mix of preheated fresh air and recirculation. This control automatically returns to full recirculation after an interval.

The aim of this is to place the responsibility for control in the hands of the users and to rely on their perceptions of the environmental conditions as the triggers for action.

The variable and unpredictable conditions of the British spring and autumn present a 'selective' environment building, and its designers, with the most difficult problem. Since the building may pass, from heat deficit to surplus and back again during a single day, the fabric and plant have to be sufficiently adaptable to cope. Under these conditions it is possible that the temperature in the conservatory will be higher than the required ambient temperature in the class spaces, thus permitting direct transfer of conservatory air to the classroom without the need for any auxiliary heating. At other times a mode similar to that in winter is adopted and, equally, there

11.5
Plan.

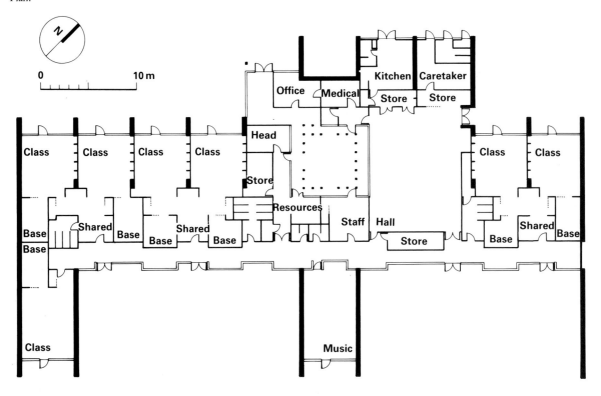

N

0          10 m

Office    Medical    Kitchen    Caretaker
                     Store      Store

Head

Class    Class    Class    Class        Class    Class

Store

Resources

Base    Shared    Base         Staff    Hall    Base    Shared    Base
Base          Base    Base                Store

Class                          Music

may be times when measures must be taken to control the temperature in the conservatory to avoid overheating.

In the summer months the building is designed to be 'free-running'. This simply means that the fabric alone can provide a comfortable environment, without any assistance from mechanical plant. The major problem with any building that uses passive solar gains in the heating season is to avoid overheating in summer. Because the conservatory acts as an environmental buffer on the south of the class spaces, these are generally protected from extreme problems of solar gain. In the transformation from heating season to summer operation the conservatory becomes the source of motive power for the stack-effect natural ventilation. The solar gains raise the temperature of the air in the conservatory and thus draw cooled outside air through the class spaces from the now openable north-facing louvres, and up out through a ridge ventilator. Excessive temperatures in the conservatory itself are avoided by the use of internal roller blinds beneath the polycarbonate glazing.

The validity of the theory of 'selective' control has been rigorously examined by a detailed monitoring study carried out for the two heating seasons 1985–86 and 1986–87.[5] In the first of these periods the results were a considerable disappointment. This was traced to malfunctions in the control systems which were rectified during the summer of 1986. The results for 1986–87 show that the system now operates in the manner intended by its designers, with a marked reduction in energy consumption (Figure 11.7). A major aim of the monitoring study was to establish the contribution made by the conservatory to the total heating requirement. The histogram, compares the actual gas consumption of the heating system with an estimate of that which would have been used if the conservatory was a source of heat loss rather than heat gain. This shows an average contribution over the heating season of 35.46%.

In its second heating season, after the first year's teething troubles had been rectified, the building consumed a total of 91 kWh/m² of delivered energy (143 kWh/m² in primary energy units). When the energy consumed in the kitchen is added the delivered total becomes 108 kWh/m². This compares with typical values from other recently completed schools in the county in excess of 200 kWh/m² of delivered energy. In money terms, this translates into savings of between £2000–£3000 per year.

These data show that a 'selective' building can achieve substantial savings in energy and, thus, provide evidence that occupant control and energy saving are not incompatible. The experience at Netley has shown that there is a necessary learning process for the users of such a building if its full potential is to be realized. There were instances, before equipment modifications, of teachers resorting to the 'cooler' setting of the mechanical ventilation system on warm

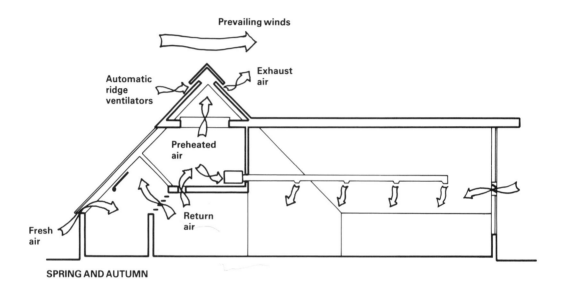

**Preheated air**

**WINTER**

**Prevailing winds**

**Automatic ridge ventilators**

**Exhaust air**

**Preheated air**

**Fresh air**

**Return air**

**SPRING AND AUTUMN**

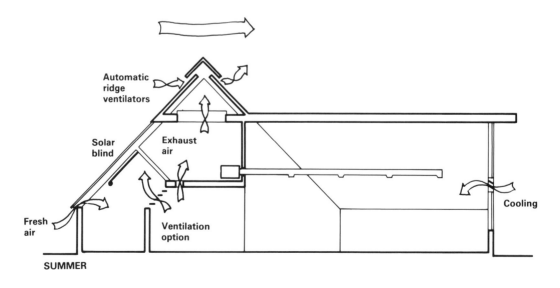

**Automatic ridge ventilators**

**Solar blind**

**Exhaust air**

**Fresh air**

**Ventilation option**

**Cooling**

**SUMMER**

138 | The Environmental Tradition

summer days, and thus drawing warm air into the classroom from the conservatory, exacerbating the problem, rather than opening the north-facing windows to activate the natural stack-effect ventilation, as the designers intended.

The major part of this discussion has, of necessity, been concerned with the environmental dimension of the building. Now this must be placed in the wider context of conventional architectural criticism.

After a period when primary school design tended towards the almost universal compact, open-plan form, the reversion to a linear configuration, which is necessitated by the passive solar dimension of 'selective' environmental design, might seem a step backwards. The pairing of class spaces with shared 'wet areas', and the use of the music room and hall to break up the sense of the traditional school corridor, successfully overcome any hint of the institutional that may lurk in the plan form. This is further sustained by the way in which the pitched roof forms bring the scale of the teaching areas down to that of the children. All of this contributes to the sense that the building makes a positive contribution to the educational process which, after all, is its *raison d'être*.

Hampshire must be given great credit for the tremendous commitment that it brought to this project and for the considerable success with which it has translated the theoretical propositions of research into concrete reality. Netley Abbey Infants' School shows that it is possible to achieve significant savings in energy consumption by exploiting the natural resource of ambient energy and, most important of all, by engaging the participation of the users in the operation of plant and hence in the control of the environment. Since all this was achieved within the county's budget for a school of this type, it is hoped that Netley is adopted as a potent exemplar for further buildings and does not suffer the heroic neglect of Emslie Morgan's pioneering solar heating at St George's School, Wallasey.

11.7
Measured performance 1986–87.

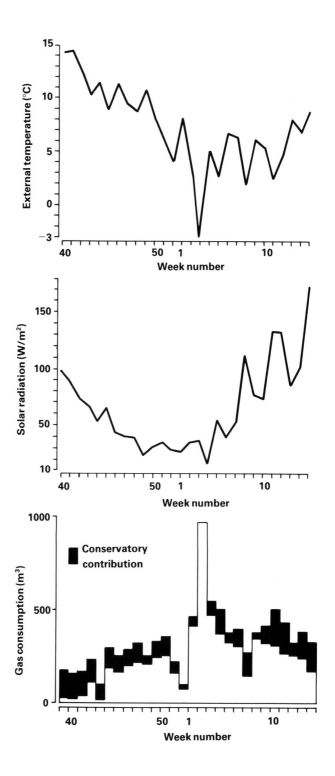

## Notes and references

1
Robson, E.R., *School Architecture*,
Leicester University Press, Leicester.
First published 1874, reprinted 1972.

2
Clay, F., *Modern School Building*,
Batsford, London, 1902.

3
Haigh, D., 'User response in
environmental control', in Hawkes, D.
and Owers, J. (eds), *The Architecture of
Energy*, Construction Press/Longman,
Harlow, 1982.

4
Baker, N., 'Atria and conservatories 2:
case study 2', *Architects' Journal*, 18
May 1983; Nelson, G., 'Schools as a
resource: what's the use of atria',
*Architects' Journal*, 20 November 1984.

5
Martin, C., 'Netley Abbey School',
monitoring report 1986–87, Energy
Monitoring Company Limited, 1987.

# 12 CEGB Building, Bristol

ARCHITECT: ARUP ASSOCIATES

12.1
Roof plan.

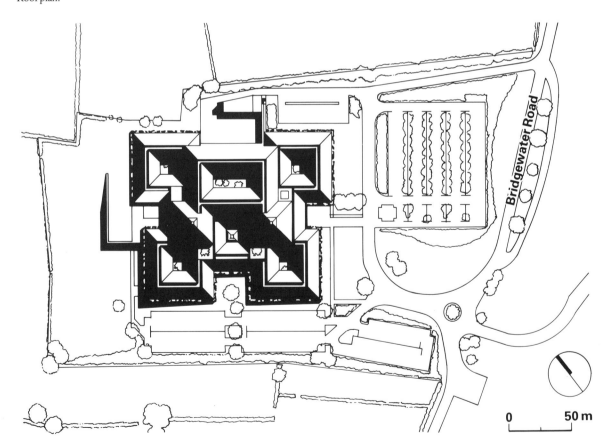

The modern office building is one of the most significant products of the theoretical and practical revolution of the modern movement. If ever form followed function and the materials and technologies of the twentieth century were comprehensively applied to a problem of architectural design, it was in the production of this building type.

A fundamental element of the type, both functionally and stylistically, is the acceptance of a highly standardized approach to environmental control. The 'kit of parts' of the deep plan, the glass wall and the suspended ceiling, from which issue the mechanical equivalents of Le Corbusier's 'sun, light and air', has become the almost inevitable norm for any office building anywhere in the world. It has created a set of standards and expectations about the physical environment within the building against which any alternative must be measured. It has also led to an aesthetic of the office environment which, because of its ubiquity, has become firmly entrenched.

On the outside, after at least two decades of conformity to the powerful model laid down by Mies van der Rohe and Philip Johnson at the Seagram Building in New York of 1959 and by Skidmore, Owings & Merrill's numerous derivatives of the 1952 Lever House in New York, there have been signs in recent years that designers have begun to recognize that the use of these advanced environmental controls actually offers total stylistic freedom. If the building is sufficiently deep and has full air conditioning and permanent artificial lighting it does not really matter what the wall looks like.

Characteristically, Philip Johnson has shown the way in this. At their technological hearts, Seagram and his infamous 'Chippendale' AT&T Building in New York of 1983 are identical. Their stylistic, and moral, contrasts are a powerful, perhaps alarming, polemic about changing attitudes in architecture. In Britain the same point can be illustrated by the comparison between RMJM's Hillingdon Civic Centre in London of 1984 and Foster Associates' building for Willis, Faber & Dumas at Ipswich of 1985. These are both deep-plan arrangements of office space and are, at the level of quantitative technical abstraction, identical. Inside and out they derive their appearance and quality from the predispositions and talents of their designers.

Arup Associates has, since the early 1960s, followed the path of modern movement righteousness. It has not been insulated from changing moods and requirements but its buildings can consistently be explained in terms of some explicit response to the programme. This is reflected not only in the buildings as technical and functional organizations, but also in their qualities and appearances. The CEGB Building of 1979 stands in this tradition. As we first perceive it, it is far removed from our preconceived

**12.2**
Detail section through office wing.

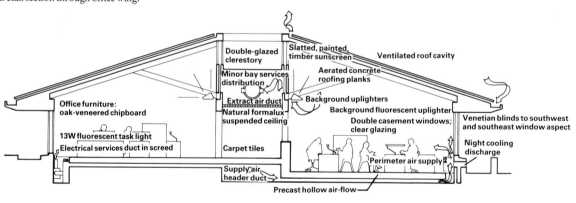

Double-glazed clerestory

Slatted, painted, timber sunscreen

Ventilated roof cavity

Minor bay services distribution

Aerated concrete roofing planks

Office furniture: oak-veneered chipboard

Extract air duct

Background uplighters

Natural formalux suspended ceiling

Background fluorescent uplighter

Double casement windows; clear glazing

Venetian blinds to southwest and southeast window aspect

13W fluorescent task light

Electrical services duct in screed

Carpet tiles

Night cooling discharge

Perimeter air supply

Supply air header duct

Precast hollow air-flow

**12.3**
Section through office wing.

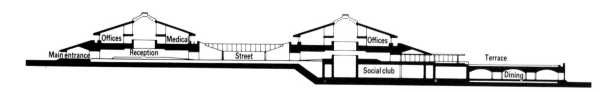

Offices

Medical

Offices

Main entrance

Reception

Street

Terrace

Social club

Dining

notions of a 'modern' building, but its 'vernacular' clothes conceal a set of values about how to design which derive quite clearly from the manifestos of the 1920s (Figure 12.1).

A peculiarly British variant on the theme of the air-conditioned, deep-plan office building is the IED (Integrated Environmental Design) type, which has been promoted by the Electricity Council. In this, the internal heat gains from lights, people and machines are brought into a calculated balance with an analysis which seeks an optimum relationship between built form and energy consumption. The advantages of the approach are that it provides a fully air-conditioned environment at relatively low capital and running costs. Its disadvantages are that it is inherently deterministic, producing a deep, squat, minimally glazed form almost regardless of contextual or other variants in the programme. In environmental terms it leads to a highly uniform environment in which control is automatic and centralized.

The CEGB Building can be presented as a reappraisal of the underlying assumptions of this approach. As in 'standard' IED, Arup has worked within the 'systems' view of environmental design, which has become the watchword of both theory and practice in recent years. This means that it has concerned itself with the complex interactions between the ends and the means of environmental control.

In establishing their environmental design intentions the architects enumerated five basic principles:

1. the amount of purchased energy should be minimized
2. maximum use should be made of natural energy sources
3. maximum use should be made of internal energy sources
4. the control of the workstation environment should be, as far as possible, on an individual or small group basis and, perhaps as a gesture to the client's vested interest
5. the broad principles of IED should be followed.[1]

In practice these principles go well beyond the conventional parameters of IED through their reference to the use of natural energy sources and their commitment to individual control over the internal environment. This allows the design to depart from the closed logic of traditional IED and opens up the possibility of a new technical and formal synthesis.

It was decided that the building should make use of natural light for a substantial part of the working year and this inevitably directed the designers' attention towards forms that allow this. The key to the environmental design thus became the cross-section through the office wing (Figure 12.2). Daylight is admitted through perimeter windows, protected from solar gain by wide eaves, and through a clerestory located above the minor bay of the structural grid. This has an internal louvred sunscreen.

## JANUARY NIGHT computer suite occupied

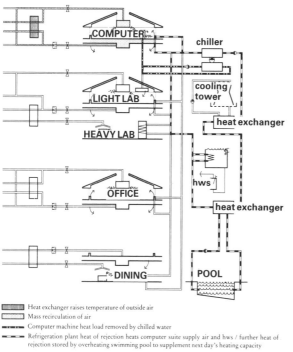

Heat exchanger raises temperature of outside air

Mass recirculation of air

Computer machine heat load removed by chilled water

Refrigeration plant heat of rejection heats computer suite supply air and hws / further heat of rejection stored by overheating swimming pool to supplement next day's heating capacity

## JANUARY DAY complete building occupied

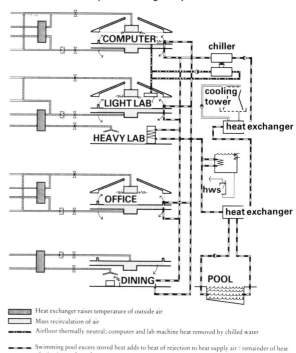

Heat exchanger raises temperature of outside air

Mass recirculation of air

Airfloor thermally neutral; computer and lab machine heat removed by chilled water

Swimming pool excess stored heat adds to heat of rejection to heat supply air / remainder of heat of rejection preheats hws

## APRIL DAY complete building occupied

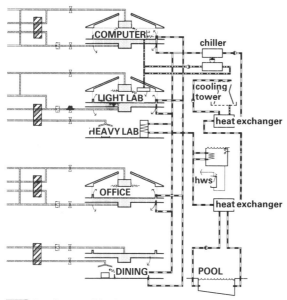

Heat exchanger on or off depending on outside air temperature

All outside air or mixed air supplied depending on outside air temperature /airfloor becomes more neutral as outside air temperature falls

Computer and lab machine heat load removed by chilled water

Refrigeration plant and process heat temper supply air / further heat of rejection preheats hws and warms pool

Any excess heat rejected through cooling tower

## APRIL NIGHT computer suite occupied

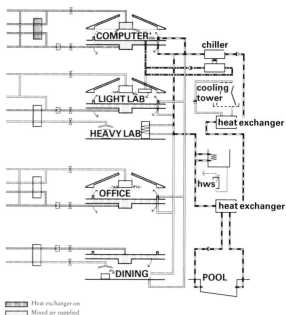

Heat exchanger on

Mixed air supplied

Precooling of airfloor reduces to zero as outside air temperature falls

Computer machine heat load removed by chilled water

Refrigeration plant heat of rejection tempers supply air / further heat of rejection maintains hws and pool temperature

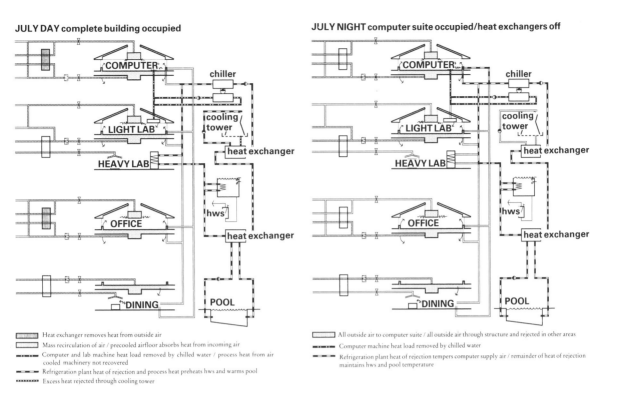

**JULY DAY complete building occupied**

COMPUTER
chiller
LIGHT LAB
cooling tower
HEAVY LAB
heat exchanger
OFFICE
hws
heat exchanger
DINING
POOL

Heat exchanger removes heat from outside air
Mass recirculation of air / precooled airfloor absorbs heat from incoming air
Computer and lab machine heat load removed by chilled water / process heat from air cooled machinery not recovered
Refrigeration plant heat of rejection and process heat preheats hws and warms pool
Excess heat rejected through cooling tower

**JULY NIGHT computer suite occupied/heat exchangers off**

COMPUTER
chiller
LIGHT LAB
cooling tower
heat exchanger
HEAVY LAB
OFFICE
hws
heat exchanger
DINING
POOL

All outside air to computer suite / all outside air through structure and rejected in other areas
Computer machine heat load removed by chilled water
Refrigeration plant heat of rejection tempers computer supply air / remainder of heat of rejection maintains hws and pool temperature

12.4
Seasonal operation diagrams.

This section is then organized into a series of pavilions, each centred upon a court. Four of these on the principal floor level accommodate the main office areas. One larger court, on the upper level, adapts the section to house a group of laboratories and associated offices. Two glazed lightwells, also at the upper level, have smaller offices located around them for special functions. It is interesting to note that in its use of the court the building returns to one of the standard elements from the early history of the office building (Figure 12.3).

Within this section and in accordance with the 'systems' view referred to above, a carefully considered set of environmental relationships is established. These seek to provide a set of conditions which are quantitatively and qualitatively quite different to those experienced in an air-conditioned office, but which offer energy savings at least equal to those of IED. General background lighting is provided naturally for much of the working year and is replaced after dark by artificial lighting which reflects off the underside of the roof and is intended only as background illumination. This is automatically controlled by a photocell-activated system which brings it into use as daylight fades. Working light comes from a specially designed and patented, individually

controlled, adjustable lamp which is an integral part of the standard desk. This is in direct response to the design intention of individual control, both functionally and, perhaps of equal importance, symbolically. In addition, staff who sit close to the windows can operate venetian blinds located between the panes of the double glazing to combat solar heat gain and glare, but the windows may not be opened for natural ventilation. The temperature control is zoned into multiples of 30 m$^2$ areas depending upon the type of occupancy.

The heating and ventilating system has a number of interesting features. Very detailed theoretical and empirical investigations, carried out with the assistance of the CEGB, showed that the thermal capacity of the building could be actively exploited to assist in temperature control in warm summer weather. In simple terms, this means that air is propelled by fans through the hollow concrete floor slabs on summer nights, cooling the structure. The next day the supply air is fed through the same structure and 'free cooling' is achieved.

In winter the structure is thermally neutral and has no effect on the normal functioning of the heating system. On a historical point, this is by no means the first use of this idea in a large building, although it is novel in the recent past. As early as 1820 the Derby Infirmary had a heating and ventilating system in which incoming air was tempered, cooled in summer and preheated in winter, by being passed along a 60 m-long underground conduit before entering the building. Above the working areas the roof construction of the CEGB Building incorporates a naturally ventilated cavity which reduces the heat gain through the structure on sunny days.

At the scale of the building as a whole, the systems' view of the process of environmental control brings all of the elements and functions into balance. The excess heat produced by the computer installation is recovered and constitutes an essential input into the system during the heating season. As in conventional IED buildings the heat produced by occupants, lighting, office machinery and plant is also recovered. The swimming pool in the social area on the lower floor is used as a heat sink when there is excess heat to be disposed of. All of this helps to reduce the need for space-consuming primary plant (Figure 12.4).

Against the background of recent office design practice the working areas at CEGB are clearly a departure and are a conscious attempt to find a new form and image. The use of natural lighting means that the variability of the external climate is sensed within the building. The articulation of the section in the interests of a good distribution of daylight means that the space and the environment within it is highly differentiated. A workplace near a window enjoys different conditions to one at the centre of the section and

there is a difference between conditions by the perimeter windows and those that look into the court (Figure 12.5 and 12.6).

The question provoked by this is, 'How does the concept perform as an office environment?' The widespread acceptance of the standardized environment of recent years may be taken to indicate that it satisfies the basic requirements of the office design programme and this implicitly challenges any alternative. But the history of architecture shows us over and over again that norms rarely have any kind of absolute authority and that they are frequently challenged and revised. In recent years the 'corporate' connotations of the 'standard' office solution have been challenged by a new image of the sociology of the organization. More technically, but deriving from the same ethos, a careful reading of the basic literature on the physiological basis of human comfort in buildings shows, in fact, that 'comfort' is a loose concept not really amenable to precise definition and, furthermore, that preferred environments are those characterized by a degree of variability, provided this is kept within bounds.

The CEGB Building is a response to this new mood and, in general environmental terms, the building is undoubtedly successful. It is very agreeable to enter an environment animated by its connection with the outside climate and which, at the same time, does not suffer from the intrusion of unwanted elements, such as excessive solar gain.

It is a pity that the design of the building envelope was not developed further to allow a response to the effects and possibilities of the different orientations which the pavilions assume. As reference to the British building tradition shows, pitched roofs offer numerous opportunities for response to be made to particular conditions. Light can be directed to places within the section with accuracy and sensitivity by the use of carefully designed dormers, and the problems of solar gain, the nightmare of postwar environmental design, can, at the same time, be easily avoided. Similar comments apply to the internal sunscreen on the clerestory, which maintains the same form on all aspects. It could have been omitted on the northerly faces and would have admitted useful additional daylighting without incurring any penalty from solar gain.

The overhang of the eaves need not be constant on all sides. On the court side, with its obstruction, it is the same as on the perimeter where the outlook is across open country. This could have been subtly and appropriately different. Outside of the classical tradition, which hardly applies here, there is nothing inherently 'regular' about the court form, as reference to Oxbridge colleges or the cloisters at Gloucester Cathedral amply demonstrates.

This kind of functionally based variation of the standard form would have introduced a useful degree of finer detail into the building and reinforced the expression of its intentions. It is hard to avoid the feeling that the architects' preoccupation with order sometimes overwhelms their appreciation of the value of variation from it, particularly in a large institutional building.

The task lighting seems to work quite well and there was ample evidence of individuals happily making the decision of how and when to use it. A few complaints were made about the lamp being in the way on the work surface, which is presumably a legacy of previous experience in generally lit spaces. One dissenting group emerged, surprisingly in view of the established use of task lighting on drawing boards, in a drawing office, where the level of background lighting was felt to be too low and has been replaced by a system of permanently used downlights supplying a high level of general lighting. This is used as the sole illumination by many of the draughtspeople and is an anachronism within the general success of the environmental scheme.

The only other individually controlled element of the local environmental system is the venetian blinds. In the general offices these can only be operated after first opening the inner pane of the double glazing. This is not difficult, but is certainly a restriction on the use of the blinds. There is a clear need for designers who contemplate user involvement in environmental control to ensure that the mode of operation is self-evident and is convenient in operation.

Regardless of one's intellectual or emotional objections to it, the main argument for the 'universal' environment of the 'standard' office solution is its ability to accommodate all office functions within a kind of technological democracy – even to the extent, occasionally, of the managing director sitting with the clerk! There is an implication in it of a levelling-up; everyone enjoys the best. By returning to a less homogeneous view of the environment in this building, Arup has made a response to a new emerging view of the aim of environmental design, with more emphasis on quality than quantity alone and accepting the new discipline of energy-conscious design. In this the architects have been successful to a substantial degree. Nonetheless, the building raises as many questions as it offers answers.

First among these is the question of how one establishes the relationship between a view about what the environment should be and the needs of the institution which occupies it. Does the urge for this new thinking reflect the aims of the organization, either corporately or individually, or does it derive from the architects' concern to develop further an abstract line of thought about design? The building is demonstrably a further step in Arup's thinking. Unlike the cosmetic stylistic gestures of some recent office buildings, the nature of this building follows from the interaction between its programme and a way of building. In this sense form follows function and 'style' derives from this.

The difference between this building and earlier 'functionally based' designs lies substantially in the redefinition of the programme. In this case it is crucial to ensure that the new programme meets the needs of the users. In my view producing an 'intimate' response to the problem of a very large building is immensely difficult. I consider that to achieve this from a wholly 'sociological' basis is impossible. It is essential that the architect should make his or her own contribution, through architecture itself.

The importance of this building lies in its demonstration that the established norms of environmental control in office buildings do not provide an absolute basis for design. In the changed circumstances following the energy price rises and our new awareness of the need to use scarce resources efficiently, it is essential that designers should seek new approaches. The basic propositions the building makes about the nature of the office environment and the means by which it may be defined should provoke new thinking about issues that have fallen into a fixed pattern in recent years.

There are, of course, many aspects of the programme and the designers' response to it that are highly specific. For example, few office buildings have the kind of relationship between office space and other facilities, such as laboratories, which has been so effectively exploited here in the organization of the environmental systems. The greenfield site also redefines many of the usual constraints on the urban office building, allowing a lower-density form and offering fewer undesirable elements of the external environment to be kept at bay. These considerations do not, however, invalidate the attractions of this building, as a fertile model for the design of office buildings. It should appeal particularly to those puritans who continue to believe in the principles of the modern movement and worry about its conventional manifestations but resist the stylistic frivolities of Johnson's 'Chippendale' design.

## Notes and references

1
These were stated in the description of the building published in the *RIBA Journal*, in June 1978.

# 13 Gateway Two, the Wiggins Teape Building, Basingstoke

ARCHITECT: ARUP ASSOCIATES

The vast majority of modern American atria, and many built in Britain, were conceived as showpieces to attract guests to hotels or tenants to speculative office buildings. Their commercial value is often the primary, maybe even the only consideration. Most are fully air-conditioned and, if anything, add to the energy consumption and running costs of the building as a whole.

However it has been argued in Britain[1] that glazed courtyards may reduce the capital cost of buildings and bestow upon them significant benefits in terms of energy savings and the creation of a high-quality internal environment. Theoretical studies have suggested that this is possible, but valid doubts remain about the precise performance of such buildings. Questions have been asked about the effectiveness of natural ventilation through atria and problems which may arise through the temperature stratification in tall spaces. There are, in addition, legitimate concerns about lighting and acoustics.

It remains the case that, for many, the real attraction of atria lies in their aesthetic and social potential, and that their technical performance is, and probably should remain, a significant but invisible bonus. The prospect of promoting social exchange by protecting 'public' space from the rigours and unpredictability of the British climate has great appeal. But the risks inherent in architectural determinism have been exposed many times. Here, even more than in the prediction of the technical performance of buildings, the only reliable guide is evidence from the real world.

In designing Gateway Two for Wiggins Teape, Arup Associates was well aware of the main technical issues. The architects set out to avoid the need for summer cooling by careful design of the external façades, incorporating fixed sunshades, and by providing thermal mass in the exposed concrete of the office ceilings. The cross-sectional depth of the office areas provides good levels of natural light in summer for most purposes – thus avoiding further heat gains from the lighting system. Ventilation was the subject of detailed computer simulations in which the stack effect of heat rising up the atrium is exploited to draw fresh air from the perimeter through the offices (Figure 13.1). Winter heating is by a straightforward hot-water system and the atrium has a low temperature underfloor system which ensures that heat is directed at the occupants at floor level and not at empty space. The atrium also benefits from a 'free' heat source, since the gain from the main-frame computer, which runs around the clock, is dumped there in winter, ensuring that the temperature is maintained at a reasonable level throughout the night (Figure 13.2).

Acoustic problems, the risk of excessive reverberation in a large volume, are dealt with by ensuring that there is enough absorbent material in the ceiling of the atrium, mainly in the form of

13.1
Atrium interior.

155 | The Wiggins Teape Building, Basingstoke

13.2
Seasonal performance diagrams: a)
section in summer, b) section in winter.

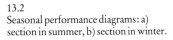

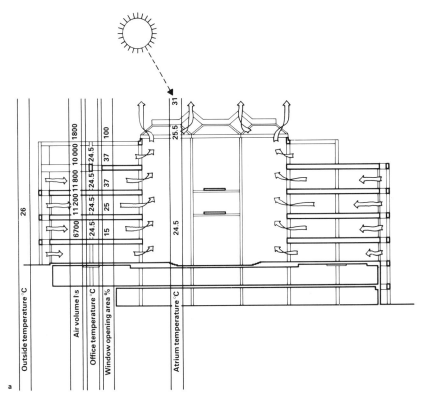

Outside temperature °C 26

Air volume l/s 6700 11 200 11 800 10 000 1800

Office temperature °C 24.5 24.5 24.5 24.5

Window opening area % 15 25 37 37 100

Atrium temperature °C 24.5 25.5 31

a

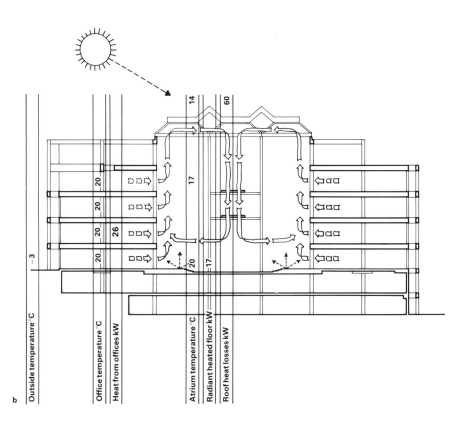

Outside temperature °C −3

Office temperature °C 20 20 20 20

Heat from offices kW 26

Atrium temperature °C 17 17

Radiant heated floor kW 14 20

Roof heat losses kW 60

b

perforated panels with a quilt backing, to keep the reverberant sound level with limits.

Commissioning of the building and its systems began in the summer of 1982 and the company moved from their 'old' Gateway One building, Arup Associates' previous, air-conditioned design of the mid-1970s, in April 1983. After the first year of use the mechanical systems and the natural ventilation have been extensively tested.

On the evidence collected, it seems that the designers' technical aims have been met. The thermal environment in the offices and the atrium is comfortable all year round, and there have been no real problems of temperature stratification, although a steep temperature gradient is unavoidable in any tall space, particularly if it has a glazed roof. By using a combination of opaque panels and internal louvres on the roof, the solar gains are kept within bounds and high temperatures have been restricted to the zone of the roof structure, where they are lowered by natural ventilation.

This must be one of the few instances where the entire staff of a large company – 550 people – have moved from a fully air-conditioned building into one with natural ventilation where they are expected to participate in the process of environmental control. In contrast to the arrangements often found in commercial buildings, it was decided to combine simple service systems with advanced controls based upon a computerized automation system. This seems to be an intelligent application of technology, achieving fine control without resort to expensive mechanized devices.

The occupants control the artificial lighting and the natural ventilation. The perimeter office areas have large pivoting opening lights and those that look into the atrium have banks of glazed louvres. Where there are cellular offices the closed doors inhibit the cross-flow of air, but in use this has not caused undue inconvenience, although initially people had to be reminded that windows can be opened.

The roof vents are pneumatically opened from a control console in the plant room when extra ventilation is required. A computer program is being developed to do this automatically in response to measurements of the difference between internal and external temperatures. Clearly this has technical advantages, but the success of the present arrangement, where the vents are opened upon occupant demand, has made the users wary of losing any of their individual control. Perhaps the two arrangements can be combined so that the automatic system looks after the building when it is unoccupied and user control is maintained in office hours. This would guarantee that heat would not build up in the enclosed atrium during hot summer weekends leading to discomfort on Monday morning.

As far as acoustics are concerned, the design is also a success. The occasional sound of distant conversation or footsteps is unobtrusive through windows open to the atrium. It is even a pleasant background sound, and certainly preferable to plant-generated white-noise. The only modification required in the first months of use has been the removal of the lift bells, whose random 'ping' was a source of annoyance.

The demonstrable technical success of the building provides the background against which we may consider the response of those who work in it. In architecture, art will always be compromised if a building fails to meet its practical objectives. That danger has been avoided here.

The visitor's first surprise will be discovering the atrium, whose presence is undeclared from outside. The experience is akin to entering Sir Charles Barry's Reform Club and finding its glazed cortile or viewing the internal courts of Kahn's Mellon Center at Yale. The sudden expansion of space and increase in light as one moves from the low-ceilinged reception area is a piece of architectural theatre. After three months of daily use the staff report that the experience continues to boost their spirits when they arrive for work each morning.

The management's growing appreciation of the building is demonstrated by the fact that some of them originally chose to have their offices on the outer edge in order to enjoy the views of the Hampshire countryside, but have now moved to the atrium side. The two high-level galleries that run the length of the atrium provide an interesting view from the offices, which would not occur if all circulation was restricted to the office areas or the atrium floor. There is a striking sense of transparency right through the building.

Already the atrium has become a focus for a wide range of uses. The company has held a series of dinner-dances, with a 15-piece band, and these have suggested the possibility of concert performances. The company rose show was held in the atrium and a snooker tournament is planned. Some of the staff have marked out a badminton court for evening use.

Word of the atrium has spread outside the company. Applications are being received from local organizations for permission to use the atrium for fund-raising events. The company has indicated that it will be willing to help with some these each year. It must be rare for a building to attract this amount of public interest, which has been inspired principally by its architectural quality.

In Gateway Two, Arup Associates has produced an exemplar for the effective design of atria in Britain's climate. The architects have shown that the theoretical arguments may be borne out in practice, providing comfortable environments throughout the year without having to use air conditioning. This should produce substantial savings in operating costs.

It also has clear material advantages, which are revealed by making a simple comparison between Gateway Two and its neighbour Gateway One. The two buildings are the same height above pavement level, but the need to provide space to accommodate a full air-conditioning system increases the floor-to-floor height of Gateway One so that it has only four storeys to Gateway Two's five. The simple hot-water heating system in Gateway Two needs no service void.

Already the atrium has become a social success. This is vital to the validity of the atrium idea. Deprived of its informal and organized uses the space would be reduced to little more than an element in an environmental control system. The purpose of technology in architecture should be to serve human needs at all levels. If this can be achieved simply and economically, it must be preferable to a display of mere machinery.

**Notes and references**

1
Hawkes, D. and MacCormac, R.,
'Office form and energy use', *RIBA Journal*, June 1978.

# 14

# St Mary's Hospital,
# Isle of Wight

### ARCHITECT: AHRENDS, BURTON & KORALEK

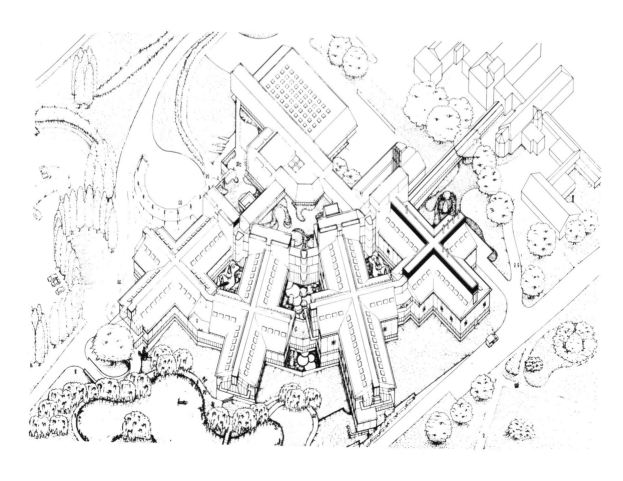

# Energy in perspective

A large modern hospital is a complex organism. A successful design has to reconcile the demands of a wide and disparate range of issues. In essence the primary purpose of a hospital is simple to define and has remained unchanged since it first emerged as a distinct building type in antiquity.[1] But the medical and social needs of modern society have led to the evolution of an elaborate set of technical and organizational requirements which form the heart of the hospital brief.

In the face of this, a great deal of effort in recent years has been devoted to developing means of simplifying and clarifying the problem as it confronts both the designers and the builders.[2] But now, because hospitals are inherently large energy users, another twist has been added to the tale. How can energy consumption be reduced, and, perhaps even more important, where does the energy question fit into the architectural hierarchy? St Mary's Hospital at Newport, Isle of Wight, 1982, is an important and serious attempt to address these questions (Figure 14.1).

In postwar Britain the existence of the National Health Service has allowed the growth of a strong tradition of research and development in hospital design. One of the most important fruits of this work has been the 'Nucleus' system of hospital planning developed by the Department of Health and Social Security. By means of a set of preplanned 'templates' for each of the main parts of a hospital and a set of overall planning rules, which also comprehend the main circulation and services distribution routes, the system seeks to relieve the designers of the need to grapple with the minutiae of departmental planning, and so allows them to concentrate on the larger questions of the specific brief and its effective arrangement on the site.

Nucleus is emphatically a *planning*, not a *building*, system. This means that, although there are certain disciplines that follow from its use, because it is essentially two-dimensional in its conception it has no explicit stylistic implications for the buildings it produces. Superimposed onto this system is a clear vertical stratification into distinct zones of 'served' and 'servant' space, in Louis Kahn's terminology. In Nucleus this is principally a simple alternating division, A-B-A-B, etc, and has none of the richness, complexity or, in some views, overelaboration of Kahn's approach to the same problem at the Richards Medical Laboratories.

What it does do, however, is to establish a number of important relationships between the parts of the building. The ratio of interior to exterior space is fixed by the dimensions of the template, and the alternation of the enclosed and open spaces, in the form of courtyards, is an inherent property of the system, as are the strictly hierarchical views of the main circulation system. In the history of

14.1
Axonometric.

161 | St Mary's Hospital, Isle of Wight

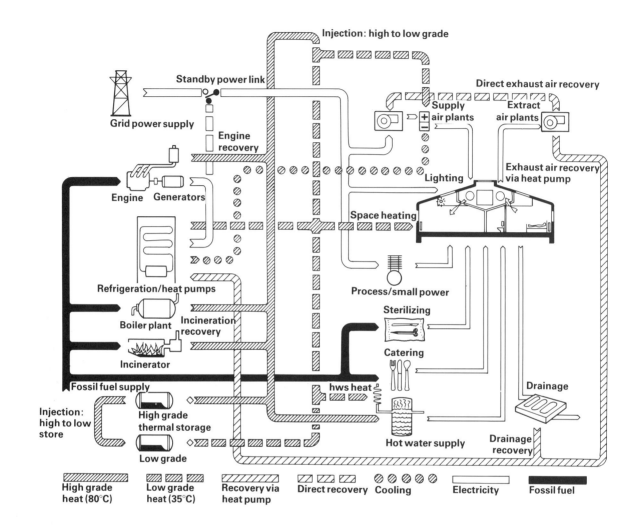

Injection: high to low grade

Standby power link

Direct exhaust air recovery

Grid power supply

Engine recovery

Supply air plants

Extract air plants

Exhaust air recovery via heat pump

Engine   Generators

Lighting

Space heating

Refrigeration/heat pumps

Process/small power

Sterilizing

Boiler plant   Incineration recovery

Catering

Incinerator

Drainage

Fossil fuel supply

hws heat

Injection: high to low store

High grade thermal storage

Hot water supply

Drainage recovery

Low grade

| High grade heat (80°C) | Low grade heat (35°C) | Recovery via heat pump | Direct recovery | Cooling | Electricity | Fossil fuel |

hospital architecture there are ample precedents for the use of standard spatial components and hierarchical planning. These supply at least the sanction of history for the underlying principles of Nucleus and who, in these days of revived historicism, can ignore that? However, we must, if we are to be true to the intentions of its authors, apply wider criteria in assessing the relevance of the system to present needs. In doing this, Ahrends Burton & Koralek's design for St Mary's Hospital at Newport on the Isle of Wight provides a near-ideal test.

Hospital buildings consume large quantities of fuel in environmental services because of their size, their continuous occupancy and the fact that they are of necessity highly serviced. When this is set against the background of the present high cost of these fuels and the financial stringency with which the NHS is faced, the case for saving energy in hospitals is compelling. As part of a series of investigations into energy conservation set up by the DHSS,[3] it has been decided to provide an active demonstration of the way forward, through the design of a number of 'exemplary' buildings. St Mary's is the first of these, and the interaction between the orthodoxy of Nucleus, the challenge of energy conservation and the freshness of approach by a firm with no previous experience of hospital building has produced a design that merits careful study.

In any consideration of energy saving in buildings we must remember that the reason for the use of energy is to achieve some standard of physical comfort. In a hospital there is a fundamental relationship between comfort and the purpose of the building. A good environment, both quantitatively and qualitatively defined, is a prerequisite of medical care. In the third edition of her *Notes on Hospitals*,[4] Florence Nightingale laid down explicit principles for the ventilation, heating and lighting of wards. There have been many changes and improvements since Nightingale's day. For example, she was able to assert with confidence that 'in England, *where fuel is cheap* [my italics], somebody is indeed to blame if the ward cannot be kept warm enough', but preoccupation with environmental conditions remains as central to hospital design today as it was for her.

The Nucleus system embodies a view of the hospital environment which is considered acceptable within the demands of current expectations, technology and costs. The aim is to achieve a balanced relationship through the form of the templates, between those parts of the hospital, mainly the wards, which require natural light and can be acceptably ventilated by natural means, and those functions which must have or can accept an artificial environment; treatment areas, operating theatres and service areas. The DHSS energy conservation study concluded that Nucleus compared favourably with the other systems evaluated. A number of possibilities which might have been considered in totally free circumstances were automatically eliminated. The approach was in many respects closer to that which would be followed in refurbishing an existing building.

The effect of this can be seen quite clearly in the procedure that was followed. Lying behind the design of St Mary's is a substantial piece of research, *The low-energy hospital study*, where the fundamental issues were extensively investigated and which, as will become clear, has had a profound influence. As a point of departure a 'model' hospital was defined, labelled 'Neutral Nucleus'. This was used by the engineering consultants to calculate a yardstick energy consumption, a 'datum', based upon clear assumptions about standards of thermal insulation, plant configuration, performance and so forth. It was established that the energy design target for the final design should be a 50% saving over Neutral Nucleus. This detailed analysis gives a clear indication of the individual components of the total energy used and reveals that 40% is consumed in hot water (19.63%) and catering (21.89%). In comparison, space heating, defined as the energy consumed by the conventionally heated perimeter zones, accounts for only 6.27%.

Armed with this information, the process of making savings could begin. An initial step was to reduce the total load through a series of 'conventional' energy-saving measures. The effect of these proposals, which have many of the characteristics of a good energy management scheme for an existing building, was to reduce the energy consumption by 28% compared with the datum of Neutral Nucleus.

A clear and conceptually useful distinction was made in the analysis between this initial phase of load reduction and a second stage in which attention was devoted to the energy left in the system. The aim here was to use techniques of heat recovery to achieve greater efficiency of use. It was calculated that these

14.3
Diagrammatic cross-section.

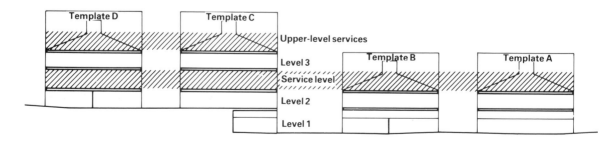

measures would produce a further 28% saving over the datum load, giving a final load of only 44% of the original.

The essentials of the final energy system are shown in Figure 14.2. It is worth noting that this is significantly different from the system of a conventional building, where energy is simply put in, used and then lost. By using heat recovery, the initial energy is retained for longer in the system and, by the expenditure of a small quantity of additional energy, is maintained in a useful condition. This allows considerable savings to be made in large hospital buildings.

It should be recorded that the studies included an assessment of the potential of solar water heating. At first sight the combination of a high, domestic, hot-water load and a sunny location in southern England might suggest that this would be an ideal application, but the analysis showed that the contribution would be marginal and certainly not cost-effective. The main reason for this is that there are other sources of cheaper low-grade energy available in a hospital, which affects the economic equation.

The discussion so far has been entirely in terms of the analysis of a hypothetical building. This establishes a series of measures which are shown to save energy. In effect, these are then added to the stock of the Nucleus system and are handed on to the designer, as is the case here. Having elected to work within the Nucleus framework, the only 'architectural' variations possible are small-scale adjustments to window sizes, the introduction of double glazing, improvements to the thermal insulation of the building and the air-tightness of the envelope. The effect of all this preliminary energy analysis on the Neutral model, even though it is logical and relevant, is to add yet more constraints.

The design of St Mary's may initially seem to have little to do with Nucleus and its orthogonal discipline. The wings of the building fan out in a quadrant and step down the south-facing slope of the site away from the main existing buildings to the north. This arrangement has a number of immediate effects. It shortens the main circulation route and breaks the standard link between the short arm of each template. The spaces between the templates are used for non-standard features such as terraces.

Great care has been taken with the planting around the building. The approach has been to seek a marriage between effect and purpose: an elaborate trellis system supports grille-growing vegetation, which is positioned to provide protection from the prevailing wind that blows across this otherwise exposed hilltop. Carefully positioned shelter belts may produce a valuable reduction in the heat loss from buildings by reducing wind speed and hence conduction and ventilation losses. The other aspect of the design in which the designers' inventiveness is most clearly shown is the development of the cross-section (Figures 14.3 and 14.4).

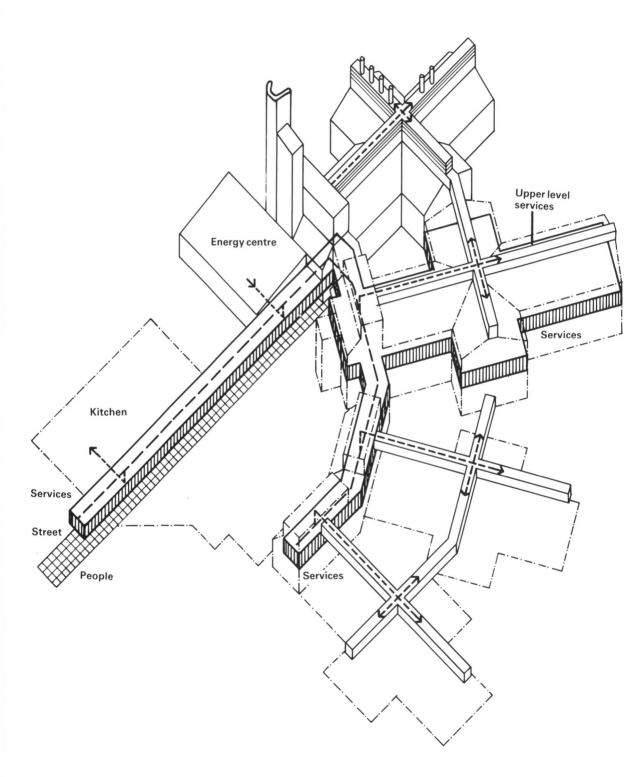

Upper level services

Energy centre

Services

Kitchen

Services

Street

People

Services

We have seen already that improvements in daylighting were one of the few architectural components of the energy analysis. What is particularly interesting is the way that qualitative concerns for the distribution of light in the building have been as important as the predominantly quantitative standards of much conventional lighting design. By moving beyond mere numerical specification, but not by abandoning it, the designers have engaged themselves explicitly in the design of the openings in the skin of the building, a relatively rare event in recent years.

The fruits of this are shown in the cross-section through the top floor wards in which a combination of windows and rooflights is used to achieve a good distribution of light throughout the wards, while keeping the problems of glare and solar gain within bounds. This kind of section has some precedents in hospital design. Henman and Cooper's Royal Victoria Hospital at Belfast, 1903, a radical building in many ways, as Reyner Banham has pointed out,[5] depended almost exclusively on top-lighting for its wards. An interesting and little-known study of hospital planning produced 70 years ago by William Atkinson[6] showed how the demands of good natural ventilation, insulation and internal relationships of wards and services could be reconciled in the manipulation of the cross-section of a ward block. More recently, Le Corbusier's project for the Venice hospital 1964–65 offered a characteristically rigorous view of the lighting of a ward cell. Ahrends, Burton & Koralek's solution is less doctrinaire than either of these and is likely to produce a comfortable and attractive environment for staff and patients.

It may come as a surprise to discover that the envelope of the building is a lightweight, stainless steel-clad frame. The conventional wisdom about the optimum thermal characteristics of continuously heated buildings suggests that a heavyweight structure is preferable. A hospital appears to be the ideal case for applying this principle, but here, as in all aspects of architectural design, the real issue is to achieve a workable compromise between several conflicting needs. The architects have given priority to achieving complete continuity of the thermal insulation of the envelope, avoiding the difficulties of cold-bridging at floor slabs, eaves and all the usual danger spots.

The roof section fulfils an important role in accommodating the main services distribution. These are all gathered together at the apex, avoiding the need to carry a suspended ceiling through from wall to wall and allowing full walling access for maintenance. Technically and visually this is a more satisfactory solution than the flat, suspended ceiling which 'standard' Nucleus produces.

The seasonal and diurnal performance of the building has been duly considered. In summer the building is 'free-running', simply relying on the envelope to modify the essentially benign external

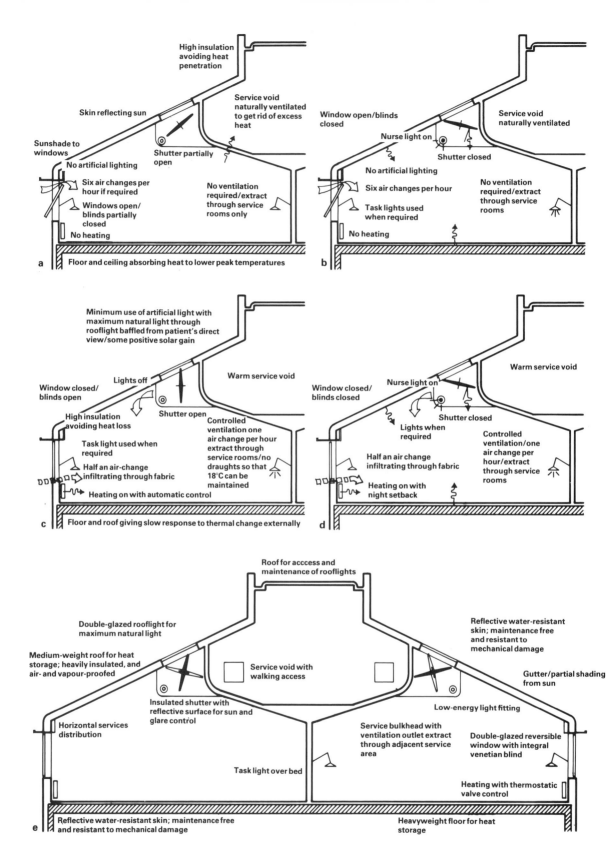

14.5
Seasonal performance diagrams:
a) typical ward – fabric performance on summer day; b) performance – summer night; c) performance – winter day; d) performance – winter night; e) cross-section through typical top-lit wards illustrating principal elements that affect building's performance.

climate. In winter, when the heating system is used, there is a shift to mechanical ventilation to control infiltration losses, to avoid discomfort from draughts and to allow the heat recovery system to be used fully (Figure 14.5).

There are a number of general points that can be made in conclusion which bear upon aspects of energy conservation and upon approaches to the design of large buildings.

In the initial aftermath of the fuel price explosion of the 1970s a great deal of attention was paid to the question of what shape was best for an energy-conserving building. Very quickly, a number of 'authorities' concluded that the 'optimum' (a dangerous word in architectural discourse) shape was one that minimized the ratio of a building's envelope to its volume – in other words, a cube-like form. As the energy question finds its place among the other concerns that form and constrain the design of a building, it is now becoming recognized that, while shape has an important bearing upon the way in which energy flows into and out of a building, it is by no means the predominant determinant of the total consumption ('Building shape and energy use' gives a more extensive discussion of this issue). Simple application of the surface area to volume criterion in the design for St Mary's Hospital would not show it in a very favourable light. But, as we have seen, its overall energy consumption is impressively low.

The combination of good engineering and thoughtful design of the building's envelope, within the dimensional and topological constraints of Nucleus, shows that the energy question can be kept in proportion. On the other hand it must be said that the sensitive elaboration of the section of the upper floors, which brings a welcome extension of the usual vocabulary of Nucleus, has clear roots in the architects' approach to saving energy used in lighting. Perhaps the lesson is to beware dogmatism in all things.

## Notes and references

1
A good survey of the history of hospital buildings can be found in Thompson. J.D. and Goldin, G., *The Hospital: a Social and Architectural History*, Yale University Press, New Haven and London, 1975.

2
'Buildings update: hospitals', *Architects' Journal*. 21 July 1982, 28 July 1982 and 18 August 1982. This series of articles gives a comprehensive review of the 'state of the art' in hospital design in the 1980s.

3
'Buildings update: hospitals', *Architects' Journal*, 28 July 1982.

4
Florence Nightingale, *Notes on Hospitals*, Longman, Brown, Green and Longmans, London, 1863.

5
Reyner Banham, *The Architecture of the Well-tempered Environment*, Architectural Press, London, 1969.

6
William Atkinson, *The Orientation of Buildings or Planning for Sunlight*, John Wiley and Sons, New York, 1912.

# 15

# Cassa Rurale e Artigianale, Brendola

ARCHITECT: SERGIO LOS

15.1
View from the southeast.

In recent years the Veneto region of northern Italy, the landscape of Palladio, has enjoyed enormous prosperity. In this still predominantly agricultural setting there has been a quiet industrial revolution. Numerous factories have grown up around the historic cities, such as Padua, Treviso and Vicenza, and along the transportation links.

To the west of Vicenza the flat hinterland of the Venice lagoon gives way to hillier terrain, and the Venice to Milan railway and autostrada are squeezed into a gap between the Monti Berici to the south and the first foothills of the Dolomites to the north.

The town of Brendola is typical of the whole region. The small historic core has been extended and transformed by industrialization. In addition to the factories themselves a substantial amount of new housing has been built, most of little architectural merit. There has also been the inevitable demand for commercial and social facilities.

A major beneficiary of this growth and prosperity has been the local bank, Cassa Rurale e Artigianale, which was originally set up to provide financial services to the agricultural community. The Italian habit of supporting local, as opposed to national or multinational, institutions has meant that the bank has been the natural resource for the new local industry. As a result its business and wealth have expanded enormously and this has led to the need for a new building (Figure 15.1).

Sergio Los built his first building, a primary school at Tarviso near Udine, in 1964, the year after he graduated from the Istituto Universitario di Architettura di Venezia (IUAV). There he was a pupil of Carlo Scarpa with whom he later collaborated on a sequence of projects from 1964–70 while he built up his own practice. Since 1978 Los has taught at the IUAV, where he is now Professor of Architectural Composition. He has continued in practice, working with his wife, Natasha Pulizer, from a studio in Bassano del Grappa to the north of Vicenza.[1]

## Act of homage

In 1967 Los published *Carlo Scarpa Architetto Poeta*,[2] one of the first works to examine Scarpa's design method in any critical detail. This focused on the design for a new entrance gate to the IUAV, which was finally realized in 1984, under the direction of Los, as an act of posthumous homage to his master.[3]

In his collaborations with Scarpa, Los worked on the project for the Carlo Felice Theatre in Genoa, the Balboni apartment in Venice, the Zentner House in Zurich, the 1964–65 project for the renovation of the Italian Pavilion at the Biennale in Venice and the De Benedetti-Bonaiuto House in Rome.

In many respects the influence of this apprenticeship can be seen in his own work from the confessional chapel at Monte Berico, Vicenza of 1969, with its 'pre-echoes' of the early works of Mario Botta, another Scarpa pupil, to a beautiful house at Olbia on Sardinia completed in 1994.

Los has not, however, seen Scarpa's work solely as a source for exquisite detail and conjunctions of extravagant materials, as have so many of his more superficial followers. Nor does he participate in the speculative, and often arcane, interpretations to which many Scarpa commentators are prone.

As with Scarpa, the work of Los has the acute sense of the way the elements of structure, material and space may be brought together, through the processes of drawing and construction, to create works of architecture that are simultaneously practical and poetic.

Los quotes Scarpa as saying:

I want to see things, that's all I really trust. I put them down in front of me on paper so that I can see them. I want to see and that's why I draw. I can see an image only if I draw it.[4]

Los has himself commented that

[Scarpa's] drawings are indeed like a musical score: they contain all the instructions needed to execute the work; they can be studied and decoded to communicate the knowledge they embody – about site, functions and building techniques. About the problem or context of the project, the drawings reveal the close relation between the work's compositional features and the constituent operations of the method followed . . . Scarpa's drawings [are] produced as a mode of thought through images rather than as a means of defining and refining elegant forms.[5]

It is commonplace for the newly successful, whether individuals or institutions, to seek architectural expression of that success. It is relatively rare for that expression to depart from current fashion. In appointing Los, the Cassa Rurale e Artigianale di Brendola was clearly prepared to break with convention.

From the outset the architect extended and redefined the programme by using this single and relatively small, building to give new and more coherent form to a site which, in spite of its evocative name of Piazza del Mercato, was a suburban parking lot. Los proposed a plan which asked the municipal authorities to undertake a planting and hard landscape scheme in which a small avenue of trees and a sequence of seats in the form of 'ruins' of an ancient city are used to suppress the impact of a drab 1960s' shopping parade with apartments above. Except for a fountain on the axis of the avenue, all the work was completed by 1990; evidence, perhaps, that the historical association between the city as artefact and civic life is still alive in Italy.

The main issue, however, is the building itself. Los' particular inheritance from Scarpa is the manner in which drawing is the essential instrument of the conception and realization of a building. In one important respect Los has added a new ingredient to Scarpa's formula – his use of computer graphics. These are not, however, a substitute for conventional drawing. Indeed Los' own drawings are extremely potent in the way they reveal the issues of a building. Drawing with the computer allows him to establish a clear image of the way in which the building is conceived and assembled as a complex set of interrelated parts and, in this, may be seen to have a direct influence on the building itself.

The programme for the bank is quite straightforward and as such is clearly reflected in the form and organization of the building. A distinction is made between the principal, public banking hall with its subsidiary spaces, which occupies the whole of the ground floor, and the more private administrative offices and boardroom on the first floor. The basement contains the plant rooms and the vault (Figures 15.2–15.5).

These simple programmatic facts play an essential role in the conception of the building. However, the form of the building is derived from a process by which questions of plan, structure and environment are explored. By a process of selection and transformation the building gradually takes shape.

Attention then turns to the details. Here, every element – roof, floor tiling, doors, internal partitions – is subjected to detailed investigation through freehand sketches, draft details and in some cases, computer projections, until the entire building is fully developed. In this way Los is personally involved in the design of every detail of the building.

The result of all this is a small building of great richness and integrity. The basic diagram is of the utmost simplicity and is declared by the strict symmetry of the east façade, which expresses the two-storey, central corridor configuration capped by a pitched roof. This figure is, however, subjected to elaborate development in both plan and section.

The banking hall, and hence the main entrance, are placed asymmetrically in the body of the building. The simplicity of the generic section is transformed by expanding the central corridor bay to form the public space, and by cutting a curved opening in the first-floor slab to establish a spatial connection with the foyer above.

Los has for many years been a major figure in the world of passive and low-energy architecture, 'bioclimatic architecture' as he prefers to call it, and these interests are strongly expressed at Brendola. The simple pitched roof is elaborated along the length of the building to direct light to the centre of the plan. The play of the alternating monopitch rooflights to the north and south upon the

173 | Cassa Rurale e Artigianale, Brendola

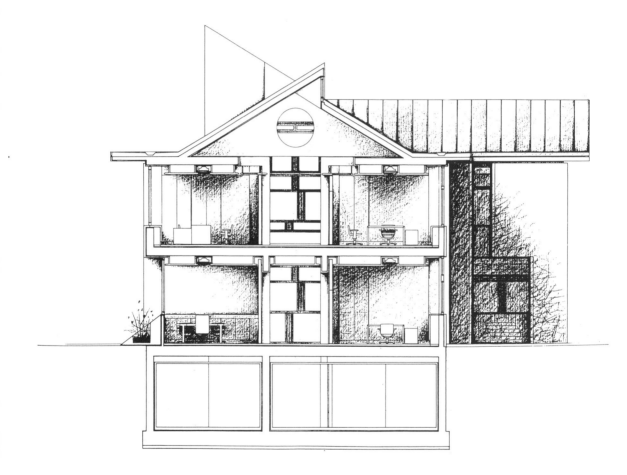

AXONOMETRIA

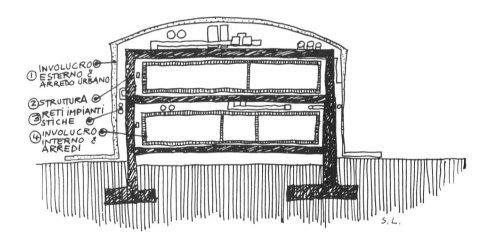

① INVOLUCRO
ESTERNO &
ARREDO URBANO

② STRUTTURA

③ RETI IMPIANTI
STICHE

④ INVOLUCRO
INTERNO &
ARREDI

S.L.

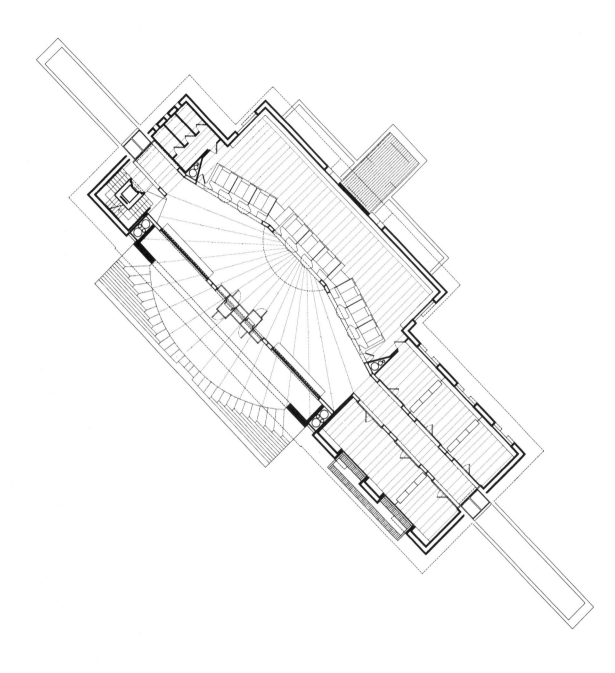

smooth white finish of the triangular roof beams, each with a circular opening at mid-span, creates a dynamic of ever-changing light and shade that animates the centre of the building. In combination with the small windows these also provide ample natural light without excessive heat gain in summer. The double-height opening above the banking hall brings top-light down to the ground floor at the deepest part of the section, and a beautifully detailed glazed ceiling admits light from the corridor at the back of the first-floor offices.

The intellectual rigour of the building is given explicit expression in the way in which it is put together, with the hierarchy of structure, roof, external walls, internal partitions clearly stated, through the selection of materials and the detailing. The insitu concrete structure is revealed on the gable elevations in the widely projecting eaves and, most clearly, in the banking hall and the central corridors where each bay is expressed by a deeply recessed junction between the paired columns and beams. Within this framework all the secondary elements – partitions, tellers' counters, balustrades – are made of elaborately detailed hardwoods, and suspended ceilings are carefully articulated where they approach the structure and finished in coloured and polished plaster (Figures 15.6–15.8).

In principle this is profoundly modernist in conception and execution, but there is one aspect of the building that seems at odds with such an analysis. Most obviously, in every sense, this is the grey reinforced concrete arch, which frames the entrance and casts its own 'shadow' on the pavement before the building. In his references to historical precedent, Los speaks of 'la facciata insegna' (façade as sign) in the work of, for example, Bernard and Durand. The clear implication is that he feels the derivation of the form of the building, from the programmatic and material facts alone, fails to adequately convey its purpose. In doing so he enters the problematic territory of postmodernism. In Robert Venturi's terminology, the 'duck' has become a 'decorated shed'. This is reinforced by the cast pattern of voussoirs and rustication on the face of the arch (Figures 15.9 and 15.10).

This departure from the logic and rigour of the rest of the building is puzzling. It is hard to believe that the entrance could not be identified, and the function of the bank not declared, by relying on the principles that so successfully inform the rest of the building. When Scarpa applied his insitu concrete façade, also a *facciata insegna*, to the Gavina showroom in Bologna, he was dealing with the problem of inserting a new use into an existing building. This is, in all respects, a different situation from that at Brendola. With Scarpa there is an absolute continuity of manner, from the applied façade through to the interior of the showroom, and, crucially, the

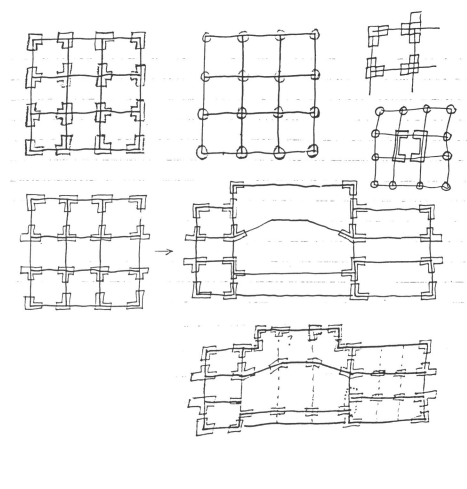

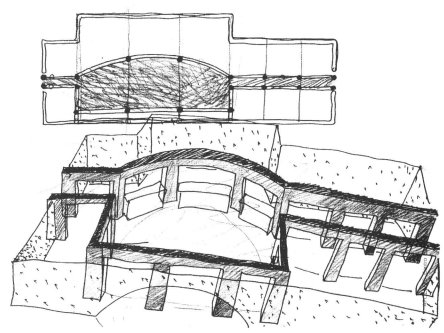

15.7
Spatial system sketch.

15.8
First-floor corridor.

15.9
Sketch showing 'Facciata insegna'.

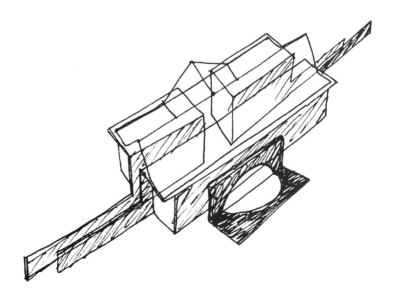

manner of the whole work is unambiguously and unashamedly carried out without resort to historicism.

This criticism concerns one of the most important questions in the present architectural debate, the expressive limitations of modernist theory and practice. In facing this apparent juxtaposition of ideologies in a single building Los is, perhaps, proposing a way forward. In principle this may well prove to be true, but I find more promise in the more subtle use of history which he demonstrates in his development of plan, structure and environmental strategies.

The lesson of Scarpa lies in the profound sense of continuity of tradition that his work exhibits, coexisting with his ability to reconsider every element of building from first principles. In the interior of the Brendola bank, Los achieves a similar synthesis. This owes a clear debt to his master, but for Los this reconsideration includes the structural clarity and the environmental conception. In this way the legacy of Scarpa lives on.

## Notes and references

1
A comprehensive review of Los' work was published in the Italian journal *Parametro*, September/October 1989.

2
Los, S., *Carlo Scarpa Architetto Poeta*, Edizioni Cluva, Venice, 1967.

3
Los, S., *Verum Ipsum Factum: il progetto di Carlo Scarpa per l'ingresso dell'Istituto Universitario di Architettura di Venezia*, Cluva Editrice, Venice 1985.

4
Quoted in Los, S., *Carlo Scarpa Architetto Poeta*, op. cit.

5
Los, S., 'The designs of the central pavilion of the Biennale', in Dal Co, F. and Mazzariol, G., *Carlo Scarpa: the Complete Works*, Electa/Architectural Press, Milan/London, 1986.

# 16

# Cambridge Crystallographic Data Centre

ARCHITECT: ERIK SØRENSON

In the great creative periods of science the scientists and the artists worked very closely together and were in many cases the same people. It was to the interest in the visual arts that we owe the birth of accurate observation of nature. It was the problems of architecture that gave rise to the science of mechanics . . . Gradually, however, with the development of bourgeois culture the useful and the ornamental were piously separated.[1]

It is a fascinating coincidence that these thoughts from an essay entitled 'Art and the scientist' were set down by J.D. Bernal who, from 1927–37, was assistant director of research in crystallography at Cambridge. Writing in 1937 he went on to show how, in the art of the twentieth century, signs could be detected of a new and potentially rich reconciliation between art and science. In the event this promise has only been realized in part. The art/science question remains high on the cultural agenda today, and nowhere, perhaps, more so than in architecture.

Against this background the Cambridge Crystallographic Data Centre building of 1992 proposes a remarkable synthesis in which architectural art and building science meet in rare harmony (Figure 16.1). In addressing a brief for a scientific institute, and particularly one in which the computer plays such a central role, it would, at first sight, have been all too easy to opt for conventional artificial lighting and full air conditioning. Instead, architect Erik Sørensen has chosen to rely on the elements of traditional daylit, naturally ventilated and centrally heated buildings, reinterpreting them in a way that answers the complex requirements of this building.

The restricted site has been turned to environmental advantage in the development of the cross-section in which the dominant element is the south-facing rooflight. This floods light on to the white-painted rear wall of the galleried principal space and this then becomes the primary light source (Figure 16.2). The fenestration of the principal, south-facing façade may then be restricted to small windows which provide specific local light to workstations (Figure 16.3). On the first floor there are six such windows. In the gallery above there are only three because of the higher level of light from the rooflight. At the east end of the first floor, light for the seminar room comes from a 2 m² louvred window and this is matched by an identical opening in the west façade. The main working area on the ground floor is lit by three pairs of large rectangular windows set deep into reveals lined with granite. A similar opening, and another of the small square lights, are found in the east façade lighting the administrative office.

This scheme of fenestration is deliberately designed to provide a lower level of natural light than is customary in working environments. This provides ideal conditions for the use of VDUs, free from the problems of specular reflection on the screens. On the other hand there is greater complexity and diversity in the distribution of light within the building as a qualitative compensation for

16.1
View from southwest.

16.2
View of the galleried interior.

16.3
Office area.

16.4
Inglenook fireplace.

the quantitative reduction. The two-storey-high vertical slit window, with its mirrored reveal, adds a degree of unpredictability by projecting surprising patches of sunlight into the space as the seasons progress.

Sørensen argues that many modern buildings are overlit and that we can function perfectly well at these lower light levels as we become accustomed to them. This challenge to accepted norms is carried through into the approach to artificial lighting where, once again, the levels of illumination are less than those recommended by the official codes. Again compensation comes from the ability of each inhabitant of the building to exercise control over the level at his or her desk. Sørensen also has a challenging view of the way in which the balance between natural and artificial lighting should be controlled. He argues that the highest levels of artificial light are required as daylight fades and that it is possible to reduce levels progressively as night falls and the eye adapts. Each of the individual desk lamps is therefore fitted with a dimmer switch.

All of this invention of thought is given its final expression in the light fittings themselves, each of which is designed by the architect and made specifically for this building by a small company in Denmark. Whatever their location or function, from the prominent fittings in the entrance hall to the lighting of basement passageways, all have been given the same fastidious attention. A final touch is the use of fibre-optic sources which sparkle, star-like, against the dark mahogany ceilings and provide the lowest level of background illumination after dark.

There is a spirit of true empiricism in the lighting philosophy of this building. Already Sørensen has responded to comments from the users by designing a new uplighter for the working areas. Most of all, however, the building should be seen as a critique of lighting design conventions, where codification has taken over from invention.

The configuration of the tall rooflight and the minimally glazed south façade is as effective in the control of the thermal environment as it is of the lighting. By eliminating undesirable solar gain from the working areas of the building, air conditioning is not required. The exposed masonry of the interior supplies useful thermal mass, and abundant stack-effect natural ventilation is provided by the opening lights in the rooflight. Incoming air enters through the louvred windows to the east and west and, as a further element of personal control, through the small windows in the south façade. The four, small, enclosed offices have mechanical ventilation provided by extract fans with ducts located in the thickness of white-painted brick partitions.

In winter, heating comes from a simple gas-fired, hot-water system, with finned-tube emitters located beneath floor grilles. The

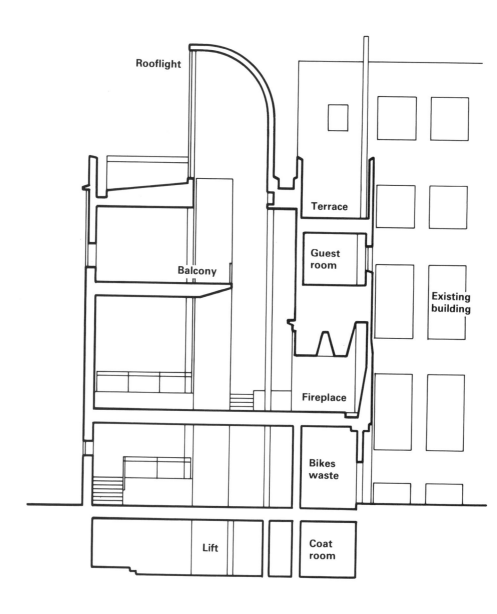

Rooflight

Terrace

Guest room

Balcony

Existing building

Fireplace

Bikes waste

Lift

Coat room

16.5
Cross-section.

188 | The Environmental Tradition

building envelope is insulated to a high standard and some useful solar gains are collected through the rooflight.

The environmental quality of the building comes from the integration of all aspects of the environment – visual, thermal and acoustic – into a seamless whole.

This synthesis follows from a grasp of the issues of environmental control which, while founded on the underlying physics and engineering of modern practice, sees the problem as one of arts as much as of science. This is most persuasively revealed in the surprising introduction of an open fire in an inglenook-like recess close to the lift on the first floor (Figures 16.4 and 16.5). This reference to domesticity and human scale is a reminder of the primal function of shelter from which all architecture derives.

This building is clearly highly specific in terms of its brief and, even more, because of the special relationship and understanding between architect and client. It should not, however, be regarded as a one-off with little to offer to other, apparently more prosaic, architectural projects.

The first lesson is that essentially simple strategies can meet the environmental demands of sophisticated modern briefs. With their modest use of renewable fuels and the inherent quality of the resultant internal environment, these methods address local and global environmental concerns. The second lesson is that conventional codified environmental specifications do not necessarily provide the only basis for design. There is still scope for working systematically from first principles to arrive at a creative restatement of the problem which then liberates the design solution. Third, the building is a powerful affirmation that art and science can work together to produce a work of originality and beauty, the useful and the ornamental reunited.

## Notes and references

1
Bernal, J.D., 'Art and the scientist', in *Circle*, Gabo, N., Martin, J.L. and Nicholson, B. (eds), Faber and Faber, London, 1937.

# 17

# The Sainsbury Wing,
# National Gallery, London

ARCHITECT: ROBERT VENTURI AND DENISE SCOTT BROWN

17.1
Robert Venturi and Denise Scott Brown,
The Sainsbury Wing, National Gallery,
London, gallery interior, 1991.

. . . I am an architect, I was a theoretician, when I was young, and had little work. I had to talk and write then to keep busy . . . But busy old architects do not theorise and probably should not . . .[1]

In this quotation from his Thomas Cubitt Lecture, delivered at the Royal Society of Arts in 1987, Robert Venturi asks to be judged by his buildings, rather than his early activities as a theoretician. The relationship between theory and practice in architecture, as in any art where there is the possibility of originality, invention, even creativity, is extremely complex. Igor Stravinsky, with characteristic waspishness, dismissed theory as 'hindsight',[2] but even he continually demonstrated his encyclopedic grasp of past and present musical theories, and their influence may be discerned throughout his *oeuvre*. Similarly it is almost inconceivable that any building that aspires to be considered a work of architecture will not bear the marks of theory, especially if its authors have themselves contributed much to the theoretical debate.

In *Learning from Las Vegas*,[3] Robert Venturi and Denise Scott Brown make much use of Alan Colquhoun's 1967 essay 'Typology and design method'[4] in developing an argument for the authority of type in the production of works of architecture and suggest, with justification, that the modern movement '[excluded] a body of traditional practice for the sake of "science" . . .' They also establish a clear position with respect to technology and function in what they term 'orthodox modern' architecture: '. . . the symbolism . . . is usually technological and functional, but when these functional elements work symbolically, they usually do not work functionally. . .'

I have chosen to approach the discussion of the Sainsbury Wing in this way because, in spite of the architects' claims, these theoretical declarations offer the only substantial basis upon which the design may be understood and assessed.

In discussing the lighting of galleries in the Kimbell Art Museum at Fort Worth, Venturi criticized Louis Kahn's approach because, in his opinion, it isn't clear whether the light is natural or artificial.[5] Kahn's invention of what he called 'this natural lighting fixture',[6] the parabolic reflectors fixed beneath the continuous rooflights at the apex of the cycloid vaults, may fall into Venturi's category of a 'functional element', but, it is surely more symbolic than functional? To avoid this paradox of 'functional elements which don't function', the galleries of the Sainsbury Wing take as their point of departure an explicit reference to the 'body of traditional practice' as it is represented in Sir John Soane's Dulwich Picture Gallery in London (Figures 17.1 and 17.2).

At Dulwich, as originally built in 1814, the vertical glazing of the monitor rooflight cast an even and controlled quantity of daylight on to the walls and pictures and, by virtue of the subtle modelling of

191 | The Sainsbury Wing, National Gallery, London

192 | The Environmental Tradition

the ceiling, the contrast between the bright sky and the interior was carefully softened. It is, in this respect, a machine for seeing pictures. The replication of this section in galleries throughout the world over the past 180 years establishes its typological authority and, no doubt, this is part of its appeal to Venturi and Scott Brown.

The superimposition of the Dulwich section on to that of the Sainsbury Wing, shows how literally the older building has influenced the new (Figure 17.3). It also reveals the extent to which fundamental demands of the modern gallery brief render the historically derived type-form only the beginning and not the end of the design process.

In his Thomas Cubitt lecture Venturi succinctly described the lighting problem:

Most museums combine daylight, with its chromatic and dynamic quality, and artificial light, with its more or less sophisticated opportunities for control and variation. And there is the important consideration today of confirming to strict conservation standards for controlling light levels and minimalising exposure to ultraviolet rays harmful to pigments . . . In lighting the galleries we must accommodate . . . contradictory requirements . . . of architecture and science.

The conservation standards also require the modern gallery, particularly one in the polluted centre of a capital city, to maintain air quality within very precisely controlled limits. Soane, building 180 years ago in a village on the outskirts of London, and innocent of the elaborate technology of modern building services engineering, could safely conceive a building in which the inside is only the thickness of a single sheet of glass away from the outside. This is no longer possible.

Many architects have tackled this problem and the range of solutions is fascinating. None of these has, however, stretched the separation of interior from exterior so far as here. Above and behind the Soanian clerestorys of the galleries there is an extensive and elaborate world of rooftop glazing. Instead of being directly connected to the galleries this glazing in fact illuminates a 'light-box' of service space from which a carefully controlled and limited quantity of daylight enters the upper parts of the galleries. The strategy of maximum separation is demonstrated, perhaps symbolized, by the systematic location of the rooflights above walls rather than spaces (Figures 17.4 and 17.5).

Within this system there are further elements of control. The air-conditioning ducts run in the *poche* above the plaster cornices of the galleries and beneath the metal decking of the light-box. All of the roof glazing has an internal, automatically controlled, louvre-blind system, which responds to outside light levels, closing when bright and opening when dull. Then there is artificial lighting. This

17.2
Sir John Soane, Dulwich Picture Gallery, London, 1814.

193 | The Sainsbury Wing, National Gallery, London

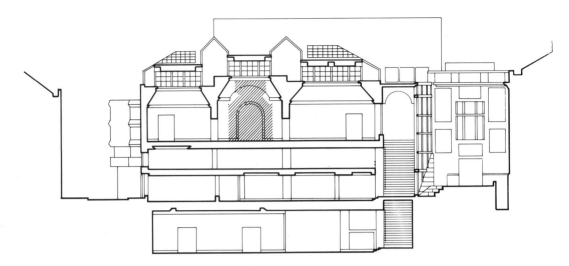

is in two parts. Beneath the louvres are continuous batteries of fluorescent tubes which create the illusion of natural light falling upon the clerestorys after dark. Then, in the ceiling coffers of the galleries and accessible from the light-box, there are the spotlights that are the actual sources of light for the pictures.

### First impressions

All of this must, finally, be judged in terms of the resultant setting for the pictures. I am usually suspicious of first impressions in architecture, preferring to give a building time. In this case, however, many visitors will see the gallery and its paintings only once, before they rejoin their coaches for 'next stop the Louvre'. So, perhaps, instant reaction is more valid than considered judgement.

On this basis I pronounce the Sainsbury Wing a major success. The paintings look terrific. Old friends, liberated from the cramped dowdiness of the original building, glow serenely in the muted calm of the new rooms. The space that each is allowed on the walls clearly assists this, but the neutrality of the grey background also seems to help project the paintings. The spatial subtlety of the plan, with its unexpected diagonals and thematic connections between paintings of different schools, and the views out to Trafalgar Square through internal windows across the great stair, are additional pleasures. The calm is undisturbed by the totally inaudible mechanical plant – a tribute to the engineering. The quality of workmanship and materials, in particular the beautiful *pietra serena* of the skirtings and architraves, are all tribute to the entire team involved in the realization of the building.

## Travels towards hyperreality

Alongside these positive responses, however, I have a feeling of unease about the building. I am reminded of Umberto Eco's devastating critique of the place of art in contemporary American culture, in which the archeological correctness and scholarship of the 'stern, learned fiercely German' display of the Getty Museum becomes almost indistinguishable from the fakery of Hearst Castle and the kitsch of the Madonna Inn, 'Arcimboldo builds the Sagrada Familia for Dolly Parton.'[7] Suddenly this seems very close to *Learning from Las Vegas* and the possibility arises that this is a decorated shed masquerading as an art gallery.

195 | The Sainsbury Wing, National Gallery, London

Since Venturi sees architecture and science as 'contradictory requirements', his programme for this, indeed any, building demands the concealment of the engineering systems and the rejection of science-derived forms, such as Alvar Aalto's parabolic reflecting surfaces in the North Jutland Art Museum project for Aalborg, in favour of Soane's historically accredited type solution. There are, however, deep contradictions in this position.

First is the fact that, as this building itself reveals, the Soanian type has to become what is in effect a stage-set within a highly serviced container if is it to provide a solution to the present problem of the urban picture gallery. The lucid certainties of Dulwich must be compromised by this. The other contradiction is that Soane's gallery section is as firmly rooted in science as anything that Aalto or Renzo Piano have proposed. Its precisely measured relationships of light source, artwork and observer reveal as much about Soane's engagement with science and technology as the mausoleum at Dulwich tells us about the Romantic movement's idealization of transcendental death. We must realize that the separation of art and science in architecture is a phenomenon of our time and our approach to architectural education. In Soane's day this would have been inconceivable.

The same question may be put in another way. When does a past solution become a typologically respectable precedent for a new building? Aalto's 'science-based' lighting system for the North Jutland Art Museum project for Aalborg was conceived in 1958. How long must we wait for it to become available to historicist architects? Or is it disqualified because the building is clearly 'orthodox modern'? If we look at the 1987 Clore Gallery at the Tate in London, we see that James Stirling and Michael Wilford's lighting system is based on a configuration not a million miles from Aalborg. It is straightened-up and related to a cellular plan but its antecedent, whether conscious or not, is quite evident (Figure 17.6). For Stirling it appears that history begins yesterday, with Venturi we have to wait longer.

All of this adds up to a commentary on the postmodern condition in general, and on its architectural consequences in particular. These picture galleries are, in fact if not in effect, a wholly artificially controlled environment for the conservation and viewing of pictures. This is achieved with great technical expertise by the engineering of the building. It must be noted, however, that the pictures are artificially lit and that the natural light which reaches the upper parts of the galleries is, in Venturi's own words, 'token'. Finally to reach the exterior of the building, the whole rooftop structure of glass is, therefore, almost wholly redundant as a light source. So we come full circle to realize that this most obviously 'functional' element of the building is, in spite of appearances, primarily symbolic.

17.5
Clerestory detail from gallery.

When the appearances and the making of a building become so separate, I can't help feeling that something fundamental to architecture is in danger of slipping from our grasp. If we go back through the history that Venturi so excitingly reappraised for us in *Complexity and Contradiction in Architecture*,[8] there are few buildings in which this disjunction is so radical. One example that has a close intellectual connection with the Sainsbury Wing is Soane's breakfast room in his London house at Lincoln's Inn Fields. The 'fantastic juxtapositions of domes and lanterns, squinches and pendentives . . .' may all be comprehended as having clear material relationships one to another to a degree which is not apparent in the Venturi building.

There is a threshold beyond which the stage-set takes over completely and where the historic nature and function of architecture, in all of its richness and genuine complexity becomes, as Eco warns, trivialized. The Sainsbury Wing remains on the right side of that line, but there are forces in contemporary society that would be quite happy for even art galleries to be shell-and-core structures, which can be refitted internally and overclad on the outside as 'needs' and fashion dictate. I'm certain Venturi and Scott Brown would not wish to be associated with that.

## Notes and references

1
Venturi, R., 'From Invention to Convention in Architecture', Thomas Cubitt Lecture, Royal Society of Arts, 8 April 1987. *RSA Journal*, January 1988.

2
Stravinsky, I. and Craft, R., *Conversations with Igor Stravinsky*, Faber Music Ltd, London, 1959.

3
Venturi, R., Scott Brown, D. and Izenour, S., *Learning from Las Vegas*, MIT Press, Cambridge, Mass., 1972.

4
Colquhoun, A. 'Typology and design method', *Arena*, June 1967. Reprinted in *Essays in Architectural Criticism*, MIT Press, Cambridge, Mass., 1981.

5
Venturi, R., news conference, Sainsbury Wing, National Gallery, London, 1 May 1991.

6
Johnson, N.E., *Light is the Theme: Louis T. Kahn and the Kimbell Art Museum*, Kimbell Art Foundation, Fort Worth, 1975.

7
Eco, U., *Travels in Hyperreality*, Pan Books. London, 1987.

8
Venturi, R. *Complexity and Contradiction in Architecture*, Museum of Modern Art, New York, 1966.

# Artistic achievements: the art museums of Louis I. Kahn

Louis Kahn's 1951 commission for the Yale University Art Gallery, New Haven, marked the turning point in his career. It was with this building that he first achieved the uncanny synthesis of form, technique and significance that was to give his later buildings their unique place in the history of architecture. He twice returned to the art museum and gallery form in the commissions for the Kimbell Art Museum at Fort Worth, 1966–72, and the Mellon Center for British Art also at Yale, 1969–74. In each scheme he embarked upon a reconsideration of the very fundamentals of the problem to arrive at a totally different solution.[1]

The initial Yale brief was for a building that would serve both as an extension to the 1920s' gallery and provide additional studio space for the school of architecture. Confronted by the indeterminacy of these requirements, the design takes the form of a very simple, four-storey block connected by a narrow link to the existing building. Each floor consists of two column-free spaces, one on either side of a central core containing services and the vertical circulation. At top-floor level this pattern is retained, disregarding the possibility of introducing any form of roof-lighting.

When the building was completed much of the critical discussion focused on the construction of the floor slabs with their system of hollow tetrahedrons through which the service installations were threaded. The *raison d'être* and origins of this system have been the subject of much discussion[2] and when, sometime later, Kahn made his now famous declaration on the distinction between 'served' and 'servant' spaces this was seen as the first clear realization of the principle in his work (Figure 18.1).

Today, from the perspective of his entire oeuvre, the building may be re-evaluated. What is striking, and of great relevance when we move on to the later buildings, is the way in which this extremely simple *parti* is transformed to achieve the 'somber and archaic tension' that Vincent Scully detected in his contemporary critique.[3] All its elements conform entirely to the principles of modernism. The structure is clearly expressed, there is no applied decoration, and the faces are either wholly glazed or wholly masonry, glazed to the north, masonry to the south.

The key element in Kahn's transformation is the inspiration to enclose the principal staircase in the concrete drum. This reaches up through the roof slab and, thus, becomes the only source of top-light in the building. The location opposite the main entrance, and adjacent to the solid south façade, establishes the drum's significance in the scheme of things at the outset and this is reinforced by continual encounters with it, glimpsed, and then entered, as one moves around the building.

The construction and finishes of this stair establish the subtle distinction of bold structure and refined detail that became one of

18.1
Louis Kahn under the Yale Art Gallery ceiling in 1953.

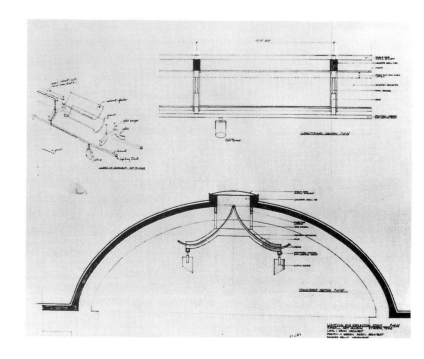

the prevailing characteristics of Kahn's mature buildings. The rough concrete sits on the black slate floor, which differentiates the core area from the maple of the loft spaces.

In 1966 Kahn received the commission for the Kimbell Art Museum. In this case the brief was unambiguously for an art museum to house the collection built up by the Kimbell Foundation since the 1930s. As usual with Kahn, the design went through a protracted process of development before it reached the severe certainty of the finished building. But, fundamental to each stage, was the idea of a deep-plan building lit through a system of rooflights and penetrated by courtyards and lightwells. The simple alternation of major and minor bays, vaults and flat roofs, served and servant spaces, is elaborated into an interior of great complexity by the placement of the courtyards.

The problem of how to control natural light under the bright, glaring Texas skies preoccupied Kahn all through the project. In a series of sketches made in March 1967, he reviewed a number of possible approaches and in one impressionistic interior perspective hinted at the final design. Two years later, precise study drawings showed how this vision was translated into reality. The parabolic reflector distributes the light which enters through the continuous rooflight onto the meticulously specified and constructed soffit of the vault. This acquires its own silvery luminosity and the whole building becomes, in Kahn's own words, a 'natural light fixture' (Figures 18.2 and 18.3).

The uniform distribution of light from the vault is transformed by the side-light that enters the gallery space from the two courtyards, the large and wholly glazed north court and the smaller south court which, being only glazed in its east and west sides admits a more sharply focused patch of light. Also, in the south wing is the conservator's courtyard whose solid enclosure penetrates through to the lower floor where it accommodates a double-height, north-facing window to the conservator's studio.

At Yale, the use of artificial light sources is the principal means of illuminating works of art, using the flexibility offered by the tetrahedral floor construction. At Kimbell, Kahn embraced the potential of natural light as a form-giver. But, as in the earlier gallery, he managed to transform a literal, actually mechanistic, lighting system, developed in a long and fruitful collaboration with the lighting consultant Richard Kelly, into an object of immense beauty.

In 1969, before the Kimbell project was complete, Kahn was given the opportunity to continue his explorations into the nature of the art museum when he was appointed to design the Mellon Center for British Art at Yale on a site directly across the street from his earlier building. Again the building was conceived as daylit, but the approach was different in almost every other respect.

18.4
Mellon Center for British Art, Yale
University, New Haven, 1974. The
reserve collection.

Much of this may be attributed to the differences between the sites and programmes of the two buildings – between open suburban at Fort Worth and restricted city centre at New Haven – and the additional demands of the academic requirements of the Mellon building. But it is more likely that Kahn felt that repetition of earlier solutions would not allow him to get at the fundamental questions the new project posed.

The building was to house Paul Mellon's collection of British art given to Yale University in 1966 and to become the focal point of an academic institution in which the accommodation for the reserve, or study, collection was to be almost as important as the public galleries. The library, including an important collection of rare books, was another significant space.

Once again the project went through an extended process of evolution and a number of highly developed proposals on the way to the final design. From the beginning Kahn developed the plan around two internal courtyards. This survived all the changes of detailed planning, structural system and numerous explorations into daylighting.

It has been suggested that a visit which Kahn made to Mellon's house to see the collection had a profound influence upon his entire approach.[4] When confronted by the bald structural expression of the exterior it may at first seem difficult to see any hint of the idea of the dwelling as an art museum. On the interior, however, a very different impression is created. In plan and section, and, most compellingly of all, on the complex play of light on surface and material, there is a sense of space and subtle recreation of the experience of a house: not of just any large house, but specifically of an English country house (Figures 18.4 and 18.5).

With the Cartesian clarity of the expressed concrete frame, a complex spatial game is played using rooms varying greatly in scale, and differing lighting conditions. The entire building is covered by a rooflight system of the utmost simplicity. Each structural bay of the building is surmounted by V-shaped concrete beams, which provide space for mechanical services and become splayed reveals to the rooflights. Each bay has four simple dome-lights which, in the picture galleries, have external metal louvres to exclude direct sunlight. Beneath are opal diffusers which further control the quantity and quality of light, rendering it, in its uniformity, closer to the relative flatness of English light under which these paintings were produced and which they frequently depict.

The interior is dominated and made coherent by the two top-lit courts to which all other spaces refer. The tall entrance court contains no pictures and therefore, requires no solar shading. The effect is to allow the dynamic quality of continuously changing patterns of light and shade to be perceived throughout the building.

As with the first Yale building, the Mellon Center's principal

18.5
Mellon Center, entrance court.

stair is contained in a concrete drum. Here, however, it has undergone a radical transformation. At the entrance level it is not fully revealed as it is approached and entered. Only on stepping out at the first floor and moving into the upper, or library court, is its dimension and nature seen. It stands free of the floor slabs and, stopping short of the roof beams, is lit through its own glass-block ceiling. The contrast between raw concrete and the refinement and finish of the oak panelling, and of the paintings themselves, further emphasizes the mysterious quality of the drum, once again 'somber and archaic'.

In 1971 Kahn said: 'When you have all the answers about a building before you start building it, your answers are not true. The building gives you answers as it grows and becomes itself.'[5] His faith in this principle is nowhere better shown than in this sequence of art museums, which precisely define the beginning and end of his late period. During these two decades he showed how, without abandoning faith in the achievements of the modern movement, without recourse to simplistic historicism or to complex extra-architectural allusion, it was possible to mould form, material and light to new expressive heights. His overriding faith was in architecture itself and this was the source of his achievement. 'You realise when you are in the realm of architecture that you are touching the basic feelings of man and that architecture would never, have been part of humanity if it weren't the truth to begin with.[6]

## Notes and references

1
Cummings Loud, P., *The Art Museums of Louis I. Kahn*, Duke University Press, Durham and London, 1989. This presents a comprehensive account of the design and construction of these buildings. I am indebted to this for much of the bibliographic information in this chapter.

2
Banham, R., 'The new brutalism', *Architectural Review*, December 1955.

3
Scully, V. 'Somber and archaic; expressive tension', *Yale Daily News*, 6 November 1953.

4
Cummings Loud, P., *op. cit.*

5
Kahn, L., in conversation with the client, 1971, reported in Johnson, N.E., *Light is the Theme: Louis I. Kahn and Kimbell Art Museum*, Kimbell Art Foundation, Fort Worth, 1975.

6
Kahn, L., lecture, Drexel Architectural Society, Philadelphia, 5 November 1968. It appeared in Wurman, R.S., *'What will be has always been': The Words of Louis I. Kahn*, Access Press and Rizzoli International Publications, New York, 1986.

# Illustration and text acknowledgements

The author and publishers would like to thank the following individuals and organizations for permission to reproduce illustrations. We have made every effort to contact and acknowledge copyright holders, but if any errors have been made we would be happy to correct them at a later printing.

Arcaid 17.6
Gabriele Basilico 15.1, 15.8, 15.10
Martin Charles 2, 6.8, 7.8, 7.9, 11.1, 11.2, 11.3, 11.4, 16.1, 16.2, 16.3, 16.4, 17.1, 17.2, 17.4, 17.5
Peter Cook 7.5, 13.1
Curteicolour 1
Leighton Gibbins 12.5, 12.6
Alastair Hunter 7.6
Leslie Martin 9.5, 9.6, 9.7, 9.8
Jeremy Preston 7.4, 10.1, 10.5
D.B. Reid 6.1
E.R. Robson 6.4

Architectural Association 7.7
Arup Associates 6.12
EMAP Business Communications 8, 6.2, 6.3, 6.5, 6.6, 6.7, 6.10, 6.11, 6.12, 6.13, 7.2, 12.4, 14.1, 14.4, 14.5, 16.5, 18.1, 18.2, 18.3, 18.4, 18.5
R. McGrath *Twentieth Century Houses*, Faber & Faber, London, 1934: 9.4
R. Giurgola and J. Menta *Louis I Kahn*, Westview Press, 1975: 6.9
Sergio Los *Un Architettura Civica: Cassa Rurale Artigiana e Piazza A Brendola*, Pagus Edizioni, 1993: 15.2, 15.3, 15.4, 15.5, 15.6, 15.7
Hicky Morgan (trans.) *Vitruvius: The Collected Works*, Harvard University Press, 1914: 4.1
Le Corbusier *Oeuvre Compléte*, Les Editions D'Architecture, Artemis, Zurich 1964: 7.1
Isaac Ware (trans.) *Quattro Libri, Andrea Palladio*, Dover Press, 1960: 4.2
Robert Tavernor *Palladio and Palladianism*, Thames & Hudson, 1991: 11, 12

Figures 4, 5, 6 and 7 are redrawn from *Design with Climate*, Victor Olgyay, Princeton University Press, 1963.
Figure 9 is redrawn with permission of Sergio Los.

We are indebted to various publishers for permission to reproduce edited versions of Dean Hawkes' previously published material:

'The theoretical basis of comfort in "selective" environments', *Energy in Buildings*, Elsevier, 1982.
'Building shape and energy use', *The Architecture of Energy*, Construction Press, 1982, Longman Group Ltd on behalf of The Martin Centre for Architectural and Urban Studies, Cambridge.
'Types, norms and habit in environmental design', *The Architecture of Form*, Cambridge University Press, March, 1976.
'Precedent and theory in the design of auditoria', *Transactions of the Martin Centre*, Martin Centre for Architectural and Urban Studies, 1980.
'Objective knowledge and the art and science of architecture', by CISA, 1989.
'Space for services: the architectural dimension', *The Architects' Journal*, EMAP Business Communications, February 1986.
'The language barrier', *The Architects' Journal*, EMAP Business Communications, March 1992.
'Environment at the threshold', *Environment for Innovation*, Rensselaer Polytechnic Institute.
'The Cambridge School and the environmental tradition' for The Martin Centre Conference, 1992.
'Wallasey School: pioneer of solar design', *The Architects' Journal*, EMAP Business Communications, May 1987.
'Netley Abbey Infants' School', *The Architects' Journal*, EMAP Business Communications, June 1988.
'CEGB Building, Bristol', *The Architects' Journal*, EMAP Business Communications, August 1979.
'Gateway Two, the Wiggins Teape Building, Basingstoke', *The Architects' Journal*, EMAP Business Communications, August 1983.
'St Mary's Hospital, Isle of Wight', *The Architects' Journal*, EMAP Business Communications, October 1982.
'Cassa Rurale e Artigianale, Brendola', *The Architects' Journal*, EMAP Business Communications, February 1992.
'Cambridge Crystallographic Data Centre', *The Architects' Journal*, EMAP Business Communications, July 1992.
'The Sainsbury Wing, National Gallery, London', *The Architects' Journal*, EMAP Business Communications, August 1991.
'Artistic Achievements: The art museums of Louis I. Kahn', *The Architects' Journal*, EMAP Business Communications, March 1992.

# Index